Introduction

As a boy, I enjoyed watching "The A-Team," an admittedly ridiculous television program in which bullets would fly, but no one—not even the bad guys—would get hit. Of course, the world isn't like silly 80's television. People do get hit with bullets. And cancer, and divorce, and infertility, and bereavement, and deep, deep depression. Thankfully, the Bible provides counsel and encouragement for hurting people. The Bible is a book about suffering, written by sufferers, for sufferers. Seriously, it's a gritty book. And that's good, because life is gritty. As D. A. Carson has said, "The truth of the matter is that all we have to do is live long enough, and we will suffer" (*How Long, O Lord*, p. 16). Perhaps you're hurting now. If so, I hope you find a balm from these meditations on the Scriptures. Perhaps you're in a time of relative ease. If so, I rejoice with you. But I also urge you to read attentively. Sooner than you think, you'll need these truths to comfort others and even to comfort yourself. Thinking biblically about suffering in the light will help you continue to think biblically in the dark, when trouble comes.

Joe Tyrpak and I were privileged to pastor together for seven years at Tri-County Bible Church in Madison, Ohio. Pastoral ministry is ministry to people who hurt. We counseled people together, wept with people together, confronted people together, prayed for people together, and buried people together. We dealt with suicides, murders, miscarriages, addictions, and marriage problems. All that to say, I've been "in the trenches" with Joe, and he's an empathizing and insightful counselor. When he first suggested that we team up again to write a devotional to help hurting people, I was very pleased. Together Joe and I have helped the hurting in person; now we're glad to help the hurting through the pages of this devotional.

Let me give a couple of disclaimers. First, we don't pretend to have all the answers. We know the Scriptures, and we're learning them. What you read here is useful only to the extent that it's biblical. So read the texts suggested for each day. Refer back to them. Check up on us. Second, we're not offering Pollyanna answers to heartbroken people. We won't tell you to grin and bear it. Were we with you, we'd probably weep with you. We won't deny that life is excruciating, and things may very well not improve during your lifetime. We won't minimize your sorrows. Finally, we're not trying to vindicate God. He's not on trial. If He were, He is more than able to answer for Himself. We're speaking on His behalf only in the sense that He has given us His inspired Word, and He's charged us to teach it with clarity and accuracy. That's our aim, by God's grace, and we believe we've done so faithfully.

Many thanks to Dan Totten, my personal friend, a stellar English teacher at Killian Hill Christian School in Lilburn, Georgia, and the editor of this book. Dan "graded" our articles— red pen and all. He vastly improved our writing, and we're deeply grateful. Dan walks with God, and he's a gifted writer. For that reason, I was pleased to ask him to contribute an article to this devotional (day seventeen). You'll be glad I did, as he writes as one who has both suffered and found succor from the gospel.

Joe and I dedicate this book to our eight children: Rebekah, Rachel, Esther, and Gracie Anderson, and Karis, Tori, Jordan, and Vera Tyrpak. Children, you've been born into a broken world. You'll suffer. Our prayer is that your sorrows will drive you to the Lord Jesus Christ, the "Man of Sorrows" who suffered like you, and for you, to bring you to God. May you know Him, love Him, and serve Him far better than your fathers have. We love you!

This is our fifth *Gospel Meditations* book, preceded by *Women, Men, Missions,* and *Prayer.* Joe and I are deeply convinced that the good news of Jesus Christ—the totality of His life, death, resurrection, ascension, and return—is the centerpiece of life. We've staked our eternity on it. We've staked our lives and livelihood on it. There is nothing about which we'd rather write, and we're thankful for the grace to help you understand, apply, and appreciate it more. May the Lord Jesus be magnified!—Chris

"For the Lord is good; his steadfast love endures forever." — PSALM 100:5

In 1998, my sister-in-law gave birth to Johnny—a sweet boy with Down Syndrome. Johnny's parents weren't expecting that their day of much-anticipated joy would also bring sorrow. They've been model parents, and he's a bright-eyed, capable Christian teenager. But those first days were difficult. Johnny had to have open heart surgery within a few months of his birth. Jeff Burr, his dad and one of my dear friends, would send out email updates, sharing the ups and downs that are inevitable at such times. At one point, Jeff started a note with these words: "God was good today. Johnny's condition improved." We understood what Jeff meant. But one of Jeff's iron-sharpening friends corrected and challenged him with this gentle reply: "God was good yesterday, too. It just didn't feel like it."

I'll never forget the wisdom of those words. God's goodness doesn't wax and wane. He's unchanging. He will never love us more, or less, than He does right now. He's constant. Even when it doesn't feel like it.

One of the great temptations we face in our seasons of discouragement is to doubt God's goodness. "If He loved me," we reason, "I would find a job. Or be healed. Or have a happy marriage. Or be more attractive. Or have better friends." We evaluate God's character based on our circumstances, when the exact opposite is in order: we should evaluate our circumstances based on God's character. A beautiful song lyric by Babbie Mason puts it this way:

> *God is too wise to be mistaken. God is too good to be unkind.*
> *So when you don't understand, when you don't see His plan,*
> *When you can't trace His hand, trust His heart.*

We can be certain of God's goodness based on repeated statements of Scripture (such as Psalm 25:8; 34:8; 84:11; 86:5). Contrary to the idols of Gentile nations (which were cruel, sensual, and debauched), God is *good*. The Bible says so. Creation declares it, even in its fallen state. History demonstrates it, despite man's cruelty. But nothing shows God's love and goodness more convincingly than the cross. That's the point of Romans 8:32, which is a response to the sorrows of life ("sufferings" in v. 18; "bondage" in v. 21; "groaning" with "pain" in vv. 22-23; "weakness" in v. 26; "tribulation, distress, persecution, famine, nakedness, danger, or sword" in vv. 35-36). When life hurts, or even ends, we must tether ourselves to the perspective of Romans 8:32: "He who did not spare his own Son but gave him up for us all, how will he not also with him graciously give us all things?"

That's a powerful, gospel-centered salve for the hurting. While we may not understand our current struggles, we can understand this: God loves us so much He sacrificed His Son to save us when we were His enemies. How unjust we are to question such infinite love! How foolish we are to doubt God's love when we lose a job (or lose our keys) or to affirm God's love when we get good news. Such thinking is mystical—and miserable. God's love is constant. The cross of Jesus Christ should put to rest any doubts about the goodness of God. You may not understand what God is doing in your life. But you know this with unshakeable certainty: God always loves you. God is only good.

I recently had the privilege of writing a hymn text for a tune written by Jonathan Hamilton, the son of Ron and Shelly Hamilton. The tune was discovered after his heartbreaking death. I took the opportunity to revel in God's constancy and goodness of which Jonathan is now certain:

> *Looking back, I can see Your fingerprints upon my life, always seeking my best.*
> *There were times when Your way would make no sense, but as You said, You have never left.*
> *You are always good, You are only good; You are always good to me.*
> *Though my eyes can't see, help my heart believe You are always, only good.*

Let the gospel assure you that God is always good—even when it doesn't feel like it.—Chris

"She is the young Moabite woman, who came back with Naomi." — RUTH 2:6

When Ruth arrived in Bethlehem, she was hurting. After a brief, childless marriage, her husband had died. She had moved away from the only home she had ever known. Now, along with her unpleasant mother-in-law, she came to a town where she was clearly an outsider. She had been left penniless, so she immediately began a life of hard manual labor in a notoriously threatening work environment just to put food on the table. The young Moabite in Bethlehem was familiar with loss, frustration, fear, marginalization, poverty, and exhaustion.

Yet the story of Ruth's life, like the life story of every believer, won't end in misery, but in the triumph of God's grace. The main point of this precious little book is that God was graciously working in the lives of Naomi, Boaz, and Ruth to raise up a much needed deliverer for His constantly failing people. The way in which God raised up that deliverer is what makes the story so engaging. Read it a hundred times, and the story never gets old: a Moabite who marries into a sinful Israelite family becomes the prime example of the virtuous woman (Ruth 3:11), the a godly man's wife (4:13), David's great-grandmother (4:17), and one whom Jesus is proud to have as part of his ancestry (Matthew 1:5). What a story of God's all-conquering grace! If you're hurting today, don't think that you're beyond the reach of God's grace. Consider Ruth.

God's grace shines in the dark. Think about Ruth's dark past. Her people were the product of Lot's incest. It's likely that she grew up worshiping the Moabite god Chemosh. She was the widow of a disobedient Israelite who had married her, an idolatrous foreigner. She had a disobedient father-in-law as well as a bitter mother-in-law who urged her to stay in Moab (Ruth 1:8-13). Don't think that "the virtuous woman" has a pristine record! Don't think that the people whom God uses are only those with childhood privileges, those who grew up in a Christian home, those who don't have "a past." *That's not Ruth.* The woman in this story never "grew up in church," and she was saved as a widowed adult! God's grace shines in the lives of sinners—sinners who are really broken, like you.

God's grace works miracles. Why did Ruth choose to commit herself to Naomi, Naomi's people, and Naomi's God (Ruth 1:14-17)? Who knows! It wasn't the attractiveness of Naomi's testimony at this time. Naomi's words in Ruth 1:15 have to rank among the worst in the history of evangelism. What made Ruth different from her Moabite sister-in-law Orpah who decided to go back home? Nothing that we can see. There's no apparent human explanation for Ruth's decisions. So where in the world did Ruth get the conviction to look Naomi in the eyes and say, "Where you go, I'll go. Where you stay, I'll stay. Your people will be my people. Your God will be my God" (1:16-17)? The answer is that God worked a gracious miracle in Ruth's heart. Just as God spoke at creation, He looked into the darkness of Ruth's heart and said, "Let there be light" (2 Corinthians 4:6). There is no life of virtue apart from God working a miracle. Hurting Christian, don't forget the amazing grace God gave you when He saved you, giving you a new heart that rejected the gods you had been living for and turned in faith to God.

God's grace endures through life. After her conversion, Ruth's life was not easy. But her life in Bethlehem was marked by years of unselfish, faithful love. No doubt, there were many days when Ruth didn't think she could keep going—work was hard, reaping was slim, sleep was short, strength was gone, and hope was dim. Yet, God gave her grace to keep going, to keep the solemn covenant she had made with Naomi. Christian, the same God who poured out His grace to sustain Ruth will sustain you. When you're worn out and feel as if you've nothing left to give, look to the God of all grace. Ask Him for more grace, and more and more still. You were saved by grace, you stand in grace, and you'll be sustained by God's all-sufficient grace.

King Jesus is proud to have Ruth as part of His family tree. And, if you're in Christ, you can call Ruth your great-grandmother, too. You have a grace-filled heritage! It's as if Jesus walks you down His palace hallways and shows you the oil paintings of His ancestors. He points out Abraham and says, "What a trophy of grace! He was an idolater from Ur." He looks at the painting of Ruth and says, "She's a trophy of grace! You should hear her story!" Then He stops the tour, turns to you, and says, "There's one thing you must know about Me: I am the King of Grace, and everyone in my kingdom testifies to it. Your life with all of its hardships will never end in despair. You'll always experience My grace, and you'll forever be a trophy of it."

Let the gospel encourage you to endure your hardships in hope.—Joe

"Cursed is the ground because of you...thorns and thistles it shall bring forth for you."
— GENESIS 3:17-18

Contrary to Louis Armstrong's iconic song, the "wonderful world" in which we live is broken. Sure, there's amazing beauty that points us to God's creativity and benevolence. But there's also cancer, poverty, natural disasters, and funerals. Why is there so much sorrow? To put the question in the words of my tearful five-year-old following a dear friend's funeral, "Why would Jesus let us die, Daddy? Doesn't he love us?" Those are tough questions. Why is "my Father's world" so full of pain?

First, we must recognize that the world which God created was good. He tells us so in Genesis 1 at the end of each of the six days of creation (vv. 4, 10, 12, 18, 21, 25). Indeed, at the end of the chapter, in verse 31, we read that God's creation was "very good." There was no sin, no suffering, no abuse, no abortion, no cancer, no death. That was God's doing.

So where did suffering come from? Well, God entrusted His perfect creation into the hands of humanity. In what we call "the Creation (or Dominion) Mandate," God charged Adam to "subdue" and exercise "dominion" over creation (Genesis 1:28; see Psalm 8:5-8). He was to "work" and "keep" Eden (Genesis 2:15). It was the perfect job, in the perfect environment. Yet, Adam rebelled against God, choosing to disobey the one prohibition God had made (Genesis 2:16-17; 3:6-7). The result of Adam's sin was catastrophic. Humanity fell in Adam, and everyone born into Adam's race (with the exception of Christ) has been tainted by sin from conception (Romans 5:12). Both the spiritual and physical death that are the wage of sin are seen immediately and tragically in Genesis 4, as Adam's son is murdered by Adam's son. From the moment Adam sinned, humanity has been both *estranged* from God (Genesis 3:8) and *exiled* from God (Genesis 3:22-24).

Adam's sin not only marred the morality of humanity but threw all of the created order under the curse. Read the consequences of sin in Genesis 3. Wildlife is cursed as a result of sin (v. 14). Satan and demons oppose us as a result of sin (v. 15). Pain is a result of sin (vv. 16a, 17). Relational conflict is a result of sin (v. 16b). Thorns and thistles are the result of sin (v. 18). Wearisome toil is a result of sin (v. 19). Death itself is the result of sin, as God promised (v. 19; 2:17). Chapter 5 of Genesis makes this point with a perpetual drumbeat of the sentence "and he died." Indeed, the book that began with "In the beginning God created" ends fifty chapters later with "They embalmed [Joseph], and he was put in a coffin in Egypt" (Genesis 50:26). In short, all the problems we face in this broken world, from disease and disaster to decay and death, are the result of humanity's failure. God gave us a perfect world—and we broke it.

The sorrow that surrounds you is man's doing. Certainly God is sovereign over all things, but mankind is culpable for sin and its effects. When you're frustrated with your fallenness (which makes sense!), point the finger at Adam and humanity, not God. The result of man's rebellion is that all creation is now groaning under the curse (Romans 8:19-22). So back to my daughter Esther's question, "Why would Jesus let us die?" The Bible answers, "Thorn and thistle." It's all about man's sin; it's all about the curse; it's all about sin's wages. And I believe that as much as death grieves us, it grieves our Lord more. It angers Him. This isn't how He created the world to be. This is a perversion of His perfect Eden. John Stott says it thus: "Suffering is an alien intrusion into God's good world" (*The Cross of Christ*, pp. 304-05).

Exactly. Suffering is an "alien intrusion," introduced by man. But it won't last forever. In the middle of the curse is the promise of the Savior who would reverse it (Genesis 3:15). We'll cover Jesus' reversal of the curse in the next study.

Let the gospel remind you of the wages of sin and of the sinner's need for a Savior.
—Chris

"Christ redeemed us from the curse of the law by becoming a curse for us." — GALATIANS 3:13

Humanity has Humpty-Dumptied the world. We received it in mint condition and were charged in the Dominion Mandate with managing it. Instead, we rebelled against God, broke the world, and can't put it back together again. What a mess.

Thankfully, God promised in Genesis 3:15 that an offspring of Eve would one day crush Satan's head, suffering pain Himself, and thereby reverse the curse. That was the mission of the Lord Jesus. According to Galatians 3:13, He came to deliver us from the curse precisely by *absorbing* the curse on our behalf. You can go line by line through Genesis 3 and see Christ's fulfillment of each portion of the curse. He suffered the pain that began in 3:16-17. He suffered the thorns that were introduced to the world in 3:18. He suffered the sweat and weariness that was promised in 3:19. He suffered the exile that was introduced in 3:24. And He suffered death, as promised in 3:19 and 2:17.

Christ's rescuing humanity from the curse is glorious. But it's not yet complete. Our bodies still die. We, along with all creation, are still "groaning" with longing for Christ's return when "the creation itself will be set free from its bondage to corruption and obtain the freedom of the glory of the children of God" (Romans 8:21). Christ's payment for sin is finished. But His reversing the curse is an ongoing, incomplete work. His work of redemption won't be finished until He has returned creation to its pre-Fall condition.

Christ is restoring the paradise we lost. That's the theme of the entire Bible. The 1,185 chapters between Genesis 1-2 and Revelation 21-22 are all telling the story of redemption. Christ is working to restore paradise. And at His return, He will. We long for the day when, in Christ's kingdom, the wolf, leopard, lion, bear, and cobra are playmates with the lamb, goat, calf, cow, and child (Isaiah 11:6-9). We long for Christ to make all things new, regenerating the heavens and earth as He has regenerated His people (Revelation 21:1-5). At that time, tears will be wiped away, death will die, and mourning and pain will be outlawed (21:4). Eden will be reclaimed and improved. The parallels between Genesis 1-2 and Revelation 21-22 are unmistakable, even including God's preparing a bride for Christ, comprised of the redeemed from the Old and New Covenants (21:9-27). Thus, as God brought Eve to the first Adam, He brings the redeemed to Christ, the second and better Adam!

But there's even more to this reclamation project. Remember the Dominion Mandate that Adam so miserably bumbled? Christ will fulfill it. Scripture records with great precision that all things will be brought under Jesus' feet at His return (Ephesians 1:22; Hebrews 2:5-8). Just as only Christ could perfectly fulfill the commands of the Law, only Christ can perfectly fulfill the Dominion Mandate. In every conceivable way, Jesus will fix this mess! Come, Lord Jesus!

I love the hope of Christ's reversing the curse. I've written of it often in ChurchWorksMedia hymns:

> *My Jesus, fair, was pierced by thorns—by thorns grown from the fall.*
> *Thus He who gave the curse was torn to end that curse for all.*
> —"My Jesus, Fair"

> *Creation groans beneath the curse—Rebellion's just reward.*
> *We long to see the fall reversed and Eden's joys restored.*
> —"Come Quickly, Lord"

> *Give glory to the Coming King, the Lord of heav'n and earth!*
> *The fallen world, like fallen men, awaits its second birth.*
> *"Behold, I shall make all things new," He promised groaning men.*
> *Dominion shall belong to Christ, and all be right again!*
> —"Give Him Glory!"

Let the gospel lift your spirit, for God's world will once again be good—very, *very* good.
—Chris

"Behold, my servant." — ISAIAH 52:13

Isaiah proclaimed God's message to Israel for six decades, including the years in which the ten northern tribes (Israel) fell to the armies of Assyria. When God first commissioned Isaiah, He told him that his messages would be largely ignored (6:9-13). According to Jewish tradition, Isaiah was killed by being sawn in half during the wicked reign of Manasseh (see Hebrews 11:37). The first thirty-nine chapters of Isaiah, "Volume 1," are primarily warnings of impending judgment. The last twenty-seven chapters, "Volume 2," are God's words of comfort to the two southern tribes (Judah) who were full of doubts regarding their present situation, fear regarding the future, and idolatry regarding the solution.

The famous prophecy of Christ in Isaiah 52:13-53:12 sits at the heart of "Volume 2." Notice God's first words: *"Behold, my servant."* Take note of God's method. How does He address trial-bound sinners who are full of unbelief, idolatry, and pride? Don't miss it! God says, *"Look at My Servant."* God addresses people who are unwilling to trust Him by pointing them to Jesus. He describes His Servant in a few dozen lines of the most powerful and moving poetry ever written. If this is God's method with unbelievers, do you think God changes His method with believers who are struggling with doubt, fear, and pride? No. God's method remains: *take a long, hard look at Jesus.* Isaiah 53 reveals five facets of His beauty.

God's Servant would be successful (52:13-15). God prophesied that the success of His Servant would be certain (52:13), surprising (52:14), and universal (52:15). In achieving this success, Jesus would act so shrewdly that His own death would be His triumph, not His defeat. His revolting appearance would cause the nations to ignore Him, then to adore Him.

God's Servant would be rejected (53:1-3). Jesus was rejected as un-believable (53:1), unimpressive (53:2), and unattractive (53:3). He didn't come looking like some dynamic politician, but like a despised and forsaken nobody. He was a man of suffering and pain, of sickness and disease, of abuse and anguish. His appearance was unattractive, but looks can be deceiving.

God's Servant would be punished in our place (53:4-6). These three verses emphasize substitution seven times. Christ would be burdened with His people's pains (53:4), pierced for their sins (53:5), and judged for their waywardness (53:6). By nature we are all self-centered. We, like shepherdless sheep, go our own way and reject the Lord's will for our lives. Yet God's Servant came, not to slaughter us, but to be slaughtered *for us!* Our rebellion fell on Him.

God's Servant would be killed (53:7-9). He was silent in His death, even though He was wrongfully abused (53:7; see Matthew 26:67-68; 27:13-14, 39-44). Jesus was ironically sentenced in His death, dying for a reason other than the charges that were brought against Him (53:8). His grave was alongside the wicked and yet somehow associated with a rich man (53:9). Who knew how this prophecy would be fulfilled?

God's Servant would be victorious (53:10-12). God desired to crush His Servant, knowing that He would come to life again. God's Servant would be raised in victory (53:10), satisfied in victory (53:11), and exalted in victory (53:12; see Philippians 2:9-11). In prophesying the Servant's satisfaction, the Lord is saying that "at the end of the day" Jesus will look over all the work He accomplished—all those whom He justified—and say, "It was totally worth it."

When God commands you to look at His Servant, He wants to show you His sovereignty and His love. God, after all, was the sole Architect of this gracious plan, and He prophesied it in remarkable detail 700 years before it happened. He acted in sovereign love so that Israel (and you) would trust Him no matter what happens. Yet, in pointing us to His Servant, the Lord also unveiled the radiance of His glory. Can you think of greater glory than what's revealed here? The One who is astonishingly disfigured is the One who astonishes the world's kings. The One whom everyone rejected is the One whom everyone needed to trust. The One whom everyone despised is the One who died for those who despised Him. The One who was violently bruised brought peace. The One who was whipped brought healing. The One whom the Lord crushed is the One in whom the Lord took great delight. The One who bore the sins of the unrighteous made sinners righteous. Believer, doesn't this glimpse of Jesus make you cry out, "Holy! Holy! Holy! Lord God Almighty! I can trust You no matter what!"

Let the gospel assure you that the God who devised it is trustworthy in every trial.—Joe

"[He] comforts us…so that we may be able to comfort others." — 2 CORINTHIANS 1:3

"I know how you feel." Those can be comforting words—or downright insulting. As a pastor, I try to empathize with people, feeling their pain even if it's foreign to me. But let's keep it real. I haven't had a miscarriage. I'm not a widow. I'm not a single parent. I haven't felt the sting of racism. I haven't endured chemotherapy. I'm not unemployed. I don't have a special-needs child. I don't have chronic pain. I'm not struggling with alcoholism. I don't fight against same-sex attraction. There are many, many afflictions that I don't understand from first-hand experience. But I thank God for those who have been there and done that, as painful as those experiences have been. God, in His infinite wisdom and goodness, has equipped the church with a diverse team of burden-bearers. How? Through comfort received and recycled, as unpacked in 2 Corinthians 1:3-7.

In our afflictions, we are comforted by God. I hope that sentence amazes you. The God who has always existed, who is infinitely transcendent, who is all-powerful, who keeps billions of people and planets from haphazardly colliding—*that God* comforts you. He comforts *you*. It's a staggering thought, and Simon J. Kistemaker rightly calls 2 Corinthians 1 "the most eloquent passage on comfort in the entire New Testament" (*New Testament Commentary: 2 Corinthians*, p. 41). It describes God the Father with the most tender of terms:

- He is "the Father of mercies" (v. 3). He is God, and He is the Father of our Lord Jesus Christ, the text says. And yet this transcendent God is also immensely immanent: He is *near*. He is *approachable*. He is *gentle*. When His children suffer (sometimes with self-inflicted sorrows), He isn't aloof or harsh or exasperated. He's merciful.

- He is "the God of all comfort" (v. 3). Let that sink in. There is no comfort outside of God. It *originates* with Him and *radiates* from Him. True, He expresses His comfort through secondary means (as we'll see below), but the comfort is His nonetheless. Our Heavenly Father doesn't relegate comfort to the Son or Spirit. He, Himself, gives to us "all comfort."

- He "comforts us in all our affliction" (v. 4a). Comfort is God's *attribute* in 1:3, and thus comfort is God's *action* in 1:4. The Comforter comforts. Notice the all-inclusive language: The God of *all* comfort comforts us in *all* our affliction. As the "catastrophe catalogues" of 2 Corinthians will reveal (4:7-12; 6:4-10; 11:23-28), that's a lot of affliction. God is aware of each anguish, each disappointment, each injustice, each heartbreak. And He comforts.

Through our afflictions, we learn to comfort others. God is multi-tasking through our trials. He comforts us for our good, but He has another end in mind as well. 2 Corinthians 1:4 says that He comforts us *in order that* (a strong statement of intent in the original Greek) we may comfort others. It's vital that you understand this. One of God's purposes for comforting you—and by extension, for ordaining your affliction in the first place—is that you might be equipped to comfort others. You take in comfort, then you pass it on. That's a consistent theme throughout Scripture. We have been forgiven, and thus we forgive (Ephesians 4:32). We have been reconciled, and thus we reconcile (2 Corinthians 5:18-20). We have been taught, and thus we teach (2 Timothy 2:2). Christian living is a chain reaction, with graces moving from one believer to the next. It's your job to perpetuate comfort. *You are not a dam, collecting God's grace. You are a pipeline, conveying it.*

Be encouraged that God is using your trial to teach you *empathy*. Those who have suffered make the best comforters. One of God's designs for your affliction is to fill out your résumé—to give you the ability to feel another's hurt. You can say, "I know how you feel," and mean it.

And be encouraged that God is using your trial to give you a *ministry*. Your pain has a purpose. God is getting you ready to help people in a way that your pastor can't. God's design for the body isn't a few "superheroes" who counsel and comfort everyone else. Rather, it's "every member ministry." God is using your present sorrow so that your church will be "staffed" to reach out to others who will have that sorrow in the future. Prepare yourself for those opportunities through prayer, Bible study, and utter dependence on God to help people as you yourself cannot.

Suffering, if not redeemed, will make you selfish. You'll meditate on your pain, or poverty, or unhappy marriage. How much better to redeem your sorrow. Look beyond yourself. Transform your self-pity into compassion and your compassion into comfort.

Let the gospel comfort you so that you can comfort others.—Chris

7 | Faith Like Concrete

"And will not God give justice to his elect, who cry to him day and night?...Nevertheless, when the Son of Man comes, will he find faith on earth?" — LUKE 18:7-8

On January 1, 2002, I stood for three hours in a line of people that wrapped several city blocks in order to see the devastation at Ground Zero in New York City. Though my feet froze, I didn't regret the wait. It's hard to describe just how vast and how messy the wreckage was. In early 2014, *Time Magazine* ran a special edition on One World Trade Center, the official name for the new single skyscraper that has replaced the fallen towers. Most people call it the Freedom Tower. With massive symbolic significance, its spire ascends 1,776 feet into the air making it (at least at the time of its opening) the tallest building in America. Of course, the most significant question that people keep asking about the building is, "How durable is it? Would it remain standing if it were attacked again?" In *Time* Josh Sanburn describes the tower's strength: "The design [of the skyscraper]...includes a bomb-resistant 20-story base set on 70-ton shafts of steel and pilings sunk some 200 ft. into the earth. This unseen subterranean structure would support 48,000 tons of steel—the equivalent of 22,500 full-size cars....The structure includes enough concrete to lay a sidewalk from Manhattan to Chicago." That's a lot of concrete. That's a solid foundation.

Luke 18 opens with two lessons from Jesus, both focusing on the kind of faith that undergirds prayer. If your life of prayer is like the skyscraper that ascends upward, your faith that undergirds it is like the deep subterranean base that sits on strong steel footers.

Your prayer life should reveal faith that's strong in perseverance. In verses 1-8 Jesus compares God with the unjust judge to show how *dissimilar* they are. Some people read this parable and assume it's teaching that they should persist in prayer, annoying God like the helpless widow so that He, like the unjust judge, will finally give in. They say, "See, we need to be persistent in praying the same thing over and over again so that we'll finally wear God out." If you think that's what this parable is teaching, you've missed the point, big-time. It's actually teaching the opposite. God is *not* like the unjust judge. He actually *cares* about you and your needs. You *don't* need to nag Him. Instead, you can be certain that He's going to answer, even though He delays. You can be certain that He's not "putting you off" (v. 7). Christian, you pray for tons of matters that seem to go unanswered. How much delay can your faith endure? This passage teaches you to persevere by remembering the just and loving character of God. Where can your faith go for a greater demonstration of God's love and justice than to the cross!

Your prayer life should reveal faith that's deep in humility. In verses 9-14 Jesus goes even deeper into the nature of Christian faith. He compares two prayers: one by a religious leader and the other by a notoriously evil man. The prayer of each man reflects his underlying faith. The Pharisee used the word *I* five times, revealing that he thought he could somehow impress God. Yet, he returned home unchanged and unforgiven. In contrast, the tax collector prayed at a distance with his eyes downcast and his fists against his chest, revealing that he believed himself to be a sinner who is embarrassed and ashamed to be in God's presence. The tax collector viewed himself as *the sinner*, the worst one. He cried out to God, literally, *"Remove Your wrath* from me!" Jesus declared that the tax collector returned home *justified*. From that moment on, God looked at the man who had a notoriously sinful past as entirely innocent on the basis of his faith. Christian, you too have been justified by God on the basis of humble, sin-admitting faith. May you never leave humility behind. May you never think that you have earned God's grace. May your prayer life never stop sounding like a needy beggar.

How durable is your faith? Will it stand through frequent attacks? Does your faith have strong perseverance and deep humility? Just like the Freedom Tower now stands where wreckage once reigned, faith that is deep and strong can make your life—once ruined by the Fall—stand as a beautiful testimony to God's grace.

Let the gospel be the concrete foundation of your life so that no trial will make you collapse. —Joe

"The Lord God has given me the tongue of those who are taught, that I may know how to sustain with a word him who is weary....I gave my back to those who strike, and my cheeks to those who pull out the beard; I hid not my face from disgrace and spitting." — ISAIAH 50:4-6

Through all the whipping and spitting and beard-ripping He endured, God's Servant paid for our sins in full, provided us an example of godly suffering, and prepared Himself for a continual ministry of encouragement to His suffering people throughout the ages. By experience God's Suffering Servant learned "how to speak a word in season to him that is weary" (Isaiah 50:4, KJV). One powerful instance of Jesus' unique ability to encourage sufferers with "a word in season" is the potent message He spoke to the persecuted church at Smyrna (Revelation 2:8-11). Learn from Jesus the kind of words that "sustain the weary."

Words about Jesus' identity sustain the weary. Jesus reminded the suffering church that He is "the First and the Last" (2:8)—the eternal God. Three times in the prophecy of Isaiah, Jehovah declares: "Thus says the LORD, 'I am the first and I am the last; besides me there is no god'" (Isaiah 41:4; 44:6; 48:12; compare Revelation 22:12-13). If you need courage in your time of suffering, remember that the Man you worship is the beginning-less, end-less God.

Words about Jesus' victory sustain the weary. Words that sustain suffering Christians must be rooted in the gospel, the message that Jesus "died and came to life" (2:8). Sufferer, Jesus died for you when you were His enemy, then He rose again to prove that there was no punishment remaining. His resurrection proved that His death was payment in full. It also proved that Jesus conquered sin and death. Weary Christian, don't worry about what could happen to you. What's the worst possibility? Death? No worry. Jesus rose, and He'll raise you.

Words about Jesus' awareness sustain the weary. Jesus knew the specifics of His church's tribulation: He knew that the church in Smyrna was poor; He knew every word of slander they had endured (2:9). Jesus is not oblivious to your trials. He knows them in great detail.

Words about Jesus' values sustain the weary. When Jesus looked at the poor, despised believers, He told them that they were rich, that they were God's true people (2:9). When Jesus looks on Christians who persevere when all they have has been taken from them, He sees faith that's much more valuable than gold that perishes (1 Peter 1:7). Suffering saint, remember that Jesus' value system is opposite the world's. He values things that eyes can't see.

Words about Jesus' counsel sustain the weary. So many times Christians don't know what to say to fellow believers in their times of trial. (And when you don't know what to say, it's always best to say nothing!) But notice that Jesus doesn't offer trite platitudes. He gives two simple admonitions: "Do not fear what you are about to suffer.... Be faithful unto death" (2:10).

Words about Jesus' sovereignty sustain the weary. Jesus knows the exact details of the future that awaits this suffering church (2:10). I think that the "ten days" of tribulation would remind this suffering church of the "ten days" when Daniel and his friends were tested as they chose not to defile themselves with the king's food (Daniel 1:14). The Smyrnan church, like Daniel, would be recognized as God's chosen and blessed people after a short time of hardship. Their trial would eventually end. Weary Christian, meditate on Jesus' sovereignty. It will sustain you.

Words about Jesus' promises sustain the weary. When believers are suffering—especially when they're on the brink of death—they need to be reminded of the eternal life Jesus promised them: "I will give you the crown of life.... The one who conquers will not be hurt by the second death" (2:10-11). If you've been delivered by God from the second death—from ever being thrown into hell (Matthew 10:28)—you have nothing to fear.

Jesus spoke *seven* kinds of encouragement in *four* short verses. These ninety words (in the original) had the power to sustain an entire congregation through the valley of the shadow of death. I'd say that Jesus, the One who suffered for us to the point of death, certainly knows "how to sustain with a word him who is weary." Christian, if you're weary, look to Jesus. If you're with someone who's weary, sustain their souls by speaking words about Jesus. Let the gospel encourage you and be the substance with which you encourage others.—Joe

"Let those who suffer according to God's will entrust their souls to a faithful Creator." — 1 PETER 4:19

If suffering comes as a surprise, it's not because God hasn't warned us. The Bible tells of Joseph's sale, Israel's bondage, Jeremiah's tears, John the Baptist's beheading, Stephen's stoning, and Paul's beatings. Yes, there were some who by faith were delivered from calamity. We highlight those grand stories from Hebrews 11. But we neglect the latter part of the chapter (vv. 35-38) where we read of people who "were tortured," who "suffered mocking and flogging, and even chains and imprisonment," who "were stoned…sawn in two…killed with the sword," who "went about in skins of sheep and goats, destitute, afflicted, mistreated." The world was unworthy of these heroes whose faith was exemplified not through miraculous deliverance but through supernatural perseverance.

God's people have always questioned why He would allow suffering. Usually His answer is that He doesn't allow suffering—He *ordains* it. Feel better? I'm guessing not. Hang in there.

In 1 Peter 4:12-19 (and indeed, throughout the whole epistle), Peter labors to encourage persecuted Christians. His words may sting a bit, but they offer relief, especially when you consider that Peter was like you—naturally averse to suffering, as his interactions with Christ often revealed. He eventually "got it."

- Even "fiery trials" shouldn't surprise us. They aren't "strange," but normal (v. 12).
- We can rejoice both at the privilege of sharing Christ's sufferings and the prospect of sharing Christ's glory (v. 13).
- When we suffer for Christ's name we do so in the power of the Holy Spirit and are thus enabled to glorify God (vv. 14-16).
- We should pity the unsaved, whose suffering will be infinitely worse than ours (vv. 17-18).
- We should trust God, for our suffering is "according to God's will" (v. 19).

There it is. Our troubles are "God's will." He doesn't just *allow* or *use* them. He *orders* them. That bothers some, and they have scrambled to explain it away. One solution was suggested by Harold Kushner in his book *When Bad Things Happen to Good People*. His view of humans is skewed; there are no "good people." But his perception of God is even worse. He hypothesizes a God who wishes evil didn't happen but is powerless to stop it. He protects God's *goodness* (he presumes) by sacrificing God's *greatness*. Proponents of "Open Theism" have done the same, postulating a God who can't know or control the future. He's nice—but impotent.

We have no right to imagine God as we want Him to be. And honestly, those answers are more troubling than the truth. Does it frighten you that God ordains even the falling of a sparrow (Matthew 10:29-31)? It shouldn't. It should *comfort* you. What alternative do you prefer: to be at the mercy of evil men? To be at the mercy of Satan? To be at the mercy of bad luck—what Shakespeare called "the slings and arrows of outrageous fortune"? No, we are far better off in the hands of a sovereign, wise, and good God, who alone ordains (and limits) our calamities.

What is God's purpose in allowing His people to suffer? Time may tell. J. C. Ryle's loss of a family fortune propelled him into ministry. John Bunyan's jail cell, intended to keep him from preaching to hundreds, allowed him to write to millions. The lice in Corrie ten Boom's quarters at Ravensbruck tormented her, but they also kept guards from discovering the Bible study she and her sister Betsie led. Jim Elliot and his fellow martyrs accomplished more for missions through their deaths than their lives. Ron Hamilton and Joni Eareckson Tada stumbled on stones that eventually became platforms for their Christ-exalting ministries.

Perhaps your own hardships will never lead to an "aha" moment. Perhaps all you'll see this side of heaven is a messy bunch of knots. But eternity will show that when your life is viewed from God's side, those knots were part of an exquisitely crafted tapestry. May we learn to handle our distresses with the faith of David Brainerd: "My soul was sweetly resigned to God's disposal of me, in every regard; and I saw there had nothing happened to me but what was best for me" (*Memoirs of Brainerd*, p. 94).

Let the gospel assure you that your suffering isn't random but is according to God's will.—Chris

"That the works of God might be displayed in him." — JOHN 9:3

"All things are ordered by the will of God, even all the sufferings and afflictions of the saints." So says John Gill, the English Baptist pastor and commentator of the eighteenth century. *Why* does God ordain afflictions? Ultimately for His glory. No text illustrates this as clearly as the healing of the blind man in John 9.

The passage begins with the disciples' debate about a man who had been born blind: "Who sinned, this man or his parents, that he was born blind" (v. 2)? Their dilemma was this: they assumed that blindness (and other afflictions) was the direct result of immediate sin. Sure, it's true that all illness stems from the fall: "thorn and thistle" (Genesis 3). But they were looking to assign blame for *this* illness to the man or his parents. "Whose fault is this?" Their view of God is a frightening one. And their view of those with diseases is a cruel one. Who's to blame when a man is "*born* blind" (a fact which is noted six times in the chapter)? Did he sin in his mother's womb? Or did his parents sin?

Such thinking is a gross misunderstanding of Scripture. It equates health with godliness and illness with sin. You'd think the book of Job would have dislodged that graceless notion millennia ago, but it survived in Jesus' day and thrives in ours. Haiti is leveled by an earthquake (it is suggested) because it has a history of witchcraft. New Orleans is submerged by a hurricane because of Mardi Gras. Soldiers are killed because some government policy has made God angry. Such Pat-Robertson-type interpreting of tragedies is selective, superstitious, and stupid. Those who suffer receive blame instead of pity. Added to their physical anguish is the mental and emotional angst of self-condemnation. I've sat across the desk from a grieving woman who assumed that every difficulty of life was the result of a teen pregnancy from almost twenty years earlier: "When will I have paid enough?"

If you're agonizing under that kind of thinking, I hope John 9:3 will be a refuge for you. Jesus teaches that the man's blindness was *not* the result of his sin or his parents'. Rather, the blindness was given *as an opportunity for God's glory*—not a punishment. God did it on purpose (see Exodus 4:11), allowing the man to have "the works of God displayed in Him." How so?

Jesus used the man's ailment to show His mercy on the afflicted. Jesus' kindness to the man shined like a diamond against the black velvet harshness of the Pharisees. They condemned him for breaking the Sabbath (or better, their perverse view of the Sabbath) rather than rejoicing in his healing (vv. 13-17). They bullied him and his parents, trying to use them against Jesus (vv. 18-23). In a shockingly ironic command, they urged the man to "give glory to God" by denouncing Jesus (v. 24). They blamed the man for his condition (v. 34). They were perfect foils, showing that God is good when men are cruel.

Jesus used the man's ailment to show His power to heal. Jesus doesn't always heal, but when He does, it's spectacular. I love how he healed this man. He spat on the ground, made mud of the saliva, then covered the man's eyes with it. Once you get past the "eww" factor, it's beautiful and ingenious. Jesus is the Creator (John 1:3). He made the worlds with a word, but He carved man out of the ground with delicacy (Genesis 2:7). Here, the Potter uses *more* ground to make a quick repair, unmistakably alluding to Genesis to show His power as the Creator.

Jesus used the man's ailment to show His grace to save. Most importantly, Jesus used the man's blindness to teach a spiritual lesson, opening his spiritual eyes to the gospel (vv. 35-38). Jesus gives spiritual sight to those who know they are blind (who repent of their sins), and He gives judicial blindness to those who claim to see (who cling to their self-righteousness; vv. 39-41).

Yes, the man suffered blindness for a time. But he also suffered blindness for a *purpose*: the glory of God. Similarly, God intends your hardships to bring Him glory. Since that is the very reason for your existence, it shouldn't matter whether you glorify Him through sickness or health, through poverty or wealth (Philippians 1:20-21). It's about Him anyway, not you. Why not pray now, thanking God for the opportunity to suffer for His glory and asking for grace to do it well?

Let the gospel inspire you to glorify God, both through comfort and conflict.—Chris

"But David remained in the wilderness." — 1 SAMUEL 26:3

First Samuel 21-24 recounts David's chaotic life "on the run" from Saul. He gets support from Abiathar in Nob, acts like a madman in Gath, escorts his parents to safety in Moab, rescues the city of Keilah from Philistine domination (before they rat him out to Saul), and then narrowly escapes Saul's attack in the wilderness. Talk about stress! The inspired historian emphasizes fifteen times that David is *in the wilderness* (23:14, 15, 24, 25; 24:2; 25:1, 4, 14, 21; 26:2, 3). Though already chosen by God and anointed by God's prophet to be King of Israel, David doesn't actually begin to reign until he's spent time being tested in the wilderness.

David's not the first believer whom God led through the wilderness. God didn't use Moses as a leader until he had spent forty years in the desert. Israel, too, began her history in the wilderness where God sustained, tested, and disciplined her for forty years (Nehemiah 9:21). Paul the Apostle endured almost fifteen years of "desert training" (Galatians 1:17-18 and 2:1). But the most profound example of wilderness preparation was the Lord Jesus, who after His public anointing was immediately "led up by the Spirit into the wilderness to be tempted by the devil" (Matthew 4:1). Like many before and after Him, Jesus' ministry didn't begin until He was tried in the wilderness. See the pattern? God puts His chosen ones through the wilderness before using them—*in order to* use them. As A. W. Tozer preached, "It is doubtful whether God can bless a man greatly until he has hurt him deeply" (*The Root of the Righteous*). God teaches His people crucial lessons in the wilderness.

In the wilderness God trains you to seek His direction. Throughout these chapters, David habitually "inquired of the Lord" (22:13, 15; 23:2, 4, 9). When David went to Ahimelech, he didn't just need bread and a sword; he needed God's direction. Throughout David's time in the desert, seeking God's direction became his lifestyle.

In the wilderness God trains you to trust His deliverance. David composed at least seven psalms during these wilderness experiences. Based on his experience in 1 Samuel 21:10-11, David wrote Psalm 56: "When I'm afraid, I put my trust in You." Based on his experience in 1 Samuel 21:13, David wrote Psalm 34. (It's ironic that this tightly ordered acrostic poem was composed around the time when David was acting like an insane madman.) Based on his experience in 1 Samuel 22:1, David wrote Psalms 57 and 142, both of which focus on God as his refuge. Based on his experience in 1 Samuel 22:9, David wrote Psalm 52 which expresses confidence that he'd never be uprooted. Based on his experience in 1 Samuel 23:14, David wrote Psalm 63, one of the greatest in the Bible's hymnbook! David knew that only God could satisfy his troubled soul. Finally, based on his experience in 1 Samuel 23:19, David wrote Psalm 54. Almost every one of these psalms ends with a deliberate choice to thank God (56:12; 57:9; 142:7; 52:9; 54:6). In the wilderness David was learning—like never before—how to choose to thank and trust in God. David's trust was expressed in and nourished through prayer. Christian, God will use your desert experience to teach you to pray. So, be a diligent student in Wilderness 101. Pray. Pray frequently. Pray aloud. Pray and sing David's wilderness psalms. Journal your prayer life. Even compose your own songs of prayer.

In the wilderness God trains you to rejoice in His provision. It was in the desert that David said goodbye to his closest friend Jonathan (23:18). Yet, David found encouragement in the company of 400 outcasts (22:2), in the prophet Gad (22:5), and in the priest Abiathar (22:20), all of whom had defected from Saul. None were people with whom David normally would have associated. They weren't strong soldiers or respectable men from the palace, but they were the people God gathered around him. Do you have any people like that in your life—outcasts with whom you normally wouldn't associate, but whom God has put around you because of your common hope in His chosen King? It's called *the church*, the ragtag family that God has given to help you endure trials. Learn to find encouragement in your God-given friends.

Christian, you may be in the wilderness. I've had a few desert experiences in my life. I reflect on them and say, "I'd never want to go back, but I wouldn't trade them for the world." That's because God trains us in the wilderness. He turns the desert into a spring.

Let the gospel encourage you to submit to God's training in the wilderness.—Joe

"Jesus said to him, 'Get up, take up your bed, and walk.'" — JOHN 5:8

The four Gospels teem with records of Jesus healing throngs of people (Matthew 4:23; 9:35). However, John 5 tells of a time when Jesus chose one seemingly random paralytic out of a throng of disabled people. Why *that* guy? Why not another? Why not all? It's an interesting miracle from which we gain a number of lessons about Jesus' help for hurting people.

Jesus is kind. Unlike many other miracles Jesus performed, this one was unsolicited. The man didn't ask for help; his parents didn't ask for help; his friends didn't ask for help. Jesus just saw the man's need and determined to meet it, regardless of the man's faith. It was an act of pure sovereign grace. This unnamed invalid had been waiting by the pool of Bethesda, hoping against hope to be healed (by who-knows-what power in the water, whether real or superstitious). Christ asked if he wanted to be healed—a rather strange question (v. 6). He responded that he had no one to assist him into the water (v. 7). Jesus did better: *"You don't need someone to carry you, and you don't need the water. Stand up and carry the bed that has heretofore carried you"* (compare v. 8).

Jesus is powerful. The man had been lame for thirty-eight years (v. 5)! (I'd like to see a so-called "faith healer" do that, rather than solving alleged headaches and back pains—all of which are invisible.) He who created the universe with but a word now cured a lame man instantaneously (v. 9) in a remarkable display of His deity (John 20:30-31).

Jesus is patient. Jesus relieved some afflictions, but not all. There was "a multitude of invalids" gathered around the pool of Bethesda that day (v. 3), but Jesus healed only one. Why? Well, His mission during His first advent was to address the root cause of suffering—*sin*. He won't alleviate all of sin's collateral damage until His second advent, which is still yet to come. He healed some as a foretaste of eternity, but He came primarily to save the sinful, not to heal the broken.

Jesus heals souls. It is remarkable that Jesus healed this man's body. It is much more remarkable that Jesus healed this man's *soul*, meeting a far greater need. Jesus, who had failed even to introduce Himself to the man at the poolside (v. 13), later sought him out in the temple (v. 14a). He told the man that being healed was good, but that being forgiven was better (v. 14b). Make no mistake: Jesus is more interested in alleviating sin than alleviating suffering—for now, at least. (Shouldn't this affect church prayer lists and missionary endeavors?) The man thought his life had been changed, and it had. But Jesus had a much larger, much longer goal in mind. What good would it do to heal the man's body only for him to run with his new legs toward eternal damnation? "Sin no more, that nothing worse may happen to you" (v. 14b). Jesus wasn't threatening the man with a worse disease; He was graciously urging the man to trust Him as Savior, lest his healed body be cast into hell (see Matthew 5:29-30; 10:28). Thirty-eight years seems like a long time, but not in light of eternity. Jesus cared more for the soul than the body, and more for eternity than time. So should we.

Why doesn't Jesus alleviate all suffering now? Why has He allowed birth defects, diseases, and deaths? For good reasons, which He alone knows. Why has He allowed your hardship? I can't tell you. But if you know Christ, I urge you to give thanks to God for meeting your greatest need through the sacrifice of the Lord Jesus. You may suffer for months, years, or even decades on earth; His grace will sustain you. But you will *not* suffer for eternity. Take heart, Christian. Your sorrow is temporary. In His infinite wisdom and mercy, Jesus has prioritized your inward man over your outward. He would rather have your body sick and your soul well than to have you healthy, carefree, and damned. That's grace.

If you don't yet know Christ as your Savior, I beg you to repent of your sins and trust Jesus now. Let your physical need push you Christ-ward for the meeting of your spiritual needs. If you will ask, Jesus will heal the malady of your soul, forgive your sins, and keep something worse from happening to you!

Let the gospel make you value your soul over your circumstances.—Chris

13 | Suicidal Thoughts: "It Is Enough" READ 1 KINGS 19

"It is enough; now, O Lord, take away my life." — 1 KINGS 19:4

Suicide is an unmentionable to many. They can't imagine getting so low that they would consider checking out. I'm glad for them. Suicide, or self-murder, should be unthinkable. But the reality is, some of the great heroes of the faith have contemplated suicide. Like whom? Like Moses (Numbers 11:14-15). Like Elijah (1 Kings 9:4). Like Job (Job 3:1-3; 7:15-16). Like Jeremiah (Jeremiah 20:14-18). Like Jonah (Jonah 4:3, 8). Perhaps like Paul, depending on whether 2 Corinthians 1:8 meant he *thought* or *hoped* he'd die. If men like that can contemplate suicide, we're foolish to avoid addressing the issue. After all, ignoring an awkward subject doesn't make it go away.

John Bunyan agrees, addressing suicide with candor in *The Pilgrim's Progress*. Christian and Hopeful (and Bunyan?) are stuck in the dungeon of Doubting Castle, tormented by Giant Despair and oppressed by want, beatings, and guilt. Giant urges them to end their suffering:

> He told them, that since they were never like to come out of that place, their only way would be forthwith to make an end of themselves, either with knife, halter, or poison; 'for why,' said he, 'should you choose to live, seeing it is attended with so much bitterness?'

Bunyan describes their agonizing struggle and eventual deliverance through the promises of God hidden in their hearts. Bunyan, the faithful pastor, thus helped his impoverished, persecuted flock, urging them to cling to the promises of God rather than tragically taking their own lives. In many respects, Bunyan portrays Elijah's condition in 1 Kings 19. We can learn much from his desire for death and from God's rescuing him from himself.

The causes of Elijah's discouragement are familiar. James 5:17 tells us that mighty Elijah was subject to the same frailties all of us are. 1 Kings 19 could be called Exhibit A. Immediately after his triumph over the prophets of Baal on Mt. Carmel, Elijah "cratered." While some of the details of his situation are miraculous and therefore unique, the basic ingredients of his suicidal despondency are timeless.

- He had just had a "mountaintop experience"—literally (ch. 18). He had won a great victory, which often yields to a great letdown. Expect it.
- He had been threatened (19:1-2). He was prepared for a religious battle, but not for the persecution it invited. The prophet who courageously opposed 450 prophets of Baal (perhaps spending all the resolve in his tank) ran from a solitary woman, wicked Jezebel.
- He had *run* from Jezebel, *fast* and *far* (19:3-4a). Exhausted in every way—physically, mentally, emotionally, and spiritually—he asked God to kill him (19:4b). Ironically, fear of death at the hand of Jezebel led him to long for death at the hand of God. Weariness is dangerous. My friend Jim Berg has often said, "I'm about as spiritual as I am rested."
- He felt alone (19:10). He avoided martyrdom, but succumbed to a martyr's complex. He assumed that all others had bowed to Baal. His solitude was cruel, and it crushed him.

God's responses to Elijah's discouragement are gracious. Too often we respond to depression by telling people to read the Bible, pray, and pull it together. We don't take the darkness of their mind and heart seriously enough. God, however, responds with tremendous compassion.

- God addressed Elijah's physical needs, giving him rest and food (19:5-7). It's worth noting that getting a checkup is a good idea in times of prolonged depression. Perhaps a physical condition is causing or contributing to your dejection. I've been there.
- God revealed Himself to Elijah (19:11-13). Communion with God will help dispel the darkness. Fight your destructive thoughts by prayerfully replacing them with Bible truth.
- God provided Elijah with human help (19:15-17). Depression thrives in solitude. Part of the answer is fellow believers, especially in the church. Don't battle suicidal thoughts in private and smile in public. Be transparent enough to seek human help!

If you're contemplating suicide, you're not the first. But you mustn't succumb to empty promises of relief. Suicide is selfish. It's murder. And it's avoidable. Ask God—and godly friends—for help. Grace to you.

Let the gospel give you the perseverance you need to live for the glory of God.—Chris

"Bless the Lord, O my soul." — PSALM 103:1, 22; 104:1, 35

Psalms 103 and 104 open and close the same way: "Bless the Lord, O my soul." The repeated command is totally comprehensive. *All* that is within me. For *all* His benefits. *All* His angels. *All* His works in *all* places of His dominion. *As long as* I live and have my being. *Every* creature in *every* place is commanded to bless the Lord with *everything* in him *every* day he lives for *every* good thing that God has done. In other words, no matter what you're going through now or what you'll face in the future, you must worship the Lord.

"Bless the Lord" is a choice. It's something you command your soul to do. Morning and evening you must summon your soul to sing over God's goodness (the general theme of Psalm 103) and God's greatness (the general theme of Psalm 104). You must sing both songs! Many people, even non-Christians, can sing one of these songs. But only true Christians can sing both. Many people can face long-term pain, major surgery, or loss believing that God is in control but that He doesn't care about their problems. They can sing Psalm 104, but not 103. On the other hand, many people can choose to sing that God is kindly empathetic but unable to control the future. They can sing Psalm 103, but not 104. Believer, you must deliberately choose to sing both of these songs every day of your life. And by God's grace, you can!

The magnificent themes of these two songs—God's goodness and greatness—are considered from three different perspectives in each psalm: from God's Word, God's creation, and God's providence in your life. In order to constantly praise God as good and great, you should be a constant student of the Scriptures, of creation, and of your own journey.

Look for evidences of God's goodness. Psalm 103 focuses on David's personal life in the first five verses. It also searches creation for illustrations of the magnitude of God's grace (vv. 11-17). But, notice how the song glories in God's grace in the biblical record. David recalls how good the Lord was to His people in the days of the Exodus (vv. 6-10). He was meditating on the Law which shows how the Lord was so faithful in His covenant love to these complaining, rebellious people. Reading Scripture about God's lovingkindness toward His people—especially in the birth, life, death, and resurrection of Jesus—should lead you to marvel at His lovingkindness toward fickle you.

Look for evidences of God's greatness. Psalm 104 focuses on the Genesis account of God's greatness (vv. 5-9) and on the writer's personal experience of God's amazing, continual provision (esp. vv. 14-15). But it focuses primarily on seeing God's greatness in the world He made. God created the sun and moon, oceans and streams, wind and thunder, mountains and valleys, fruits and grains, lions and humans, flying things and creeping things and swimming things. There's enough proof of God's greatness in creation to fill our hearts with wonder for a thousand lifetimes. A few years ago I visited the Van Andel Museum in Grand Rapids, Michigan. There I climbed two flights of stairs and stood right next to the skeleton of a seventy-six-foot fin whale that was hanging from the ceiling. The whale's jaw bone (from the center of the chin to the hinge) was twenty feet long. What a fearfully awesome creature! And that is just one of more than 20,000 species of sea creatures. Studying creation should lead us to say, "God, You're remarkable! You're awesome!" Here's some practical advice: next time you're depressed, visit a park or museum, think about how the wonders you see display God's greatness, and keep a journal of your thoughts. Such activities, marinated in Scripture, will help you keep your heart filled with fresh wonder at God's greatness.

Psalm 104 ends, "Let sinners be consumed from the earth." If you're God's creature, enjoying God's health, surrounded by God's beauty, eating God's food, breathing God's air, but you've never chosen to deny yourself and follow the Lord Jesus, you need to repent before it's too late and you're consumed from God's earth. Jesus is the great Creator who in loving goodness made Himself a sacrifice for your sins. He's the only human who ever worshiped God His Father with all His heart 24/7/365. And yet He was condemned in the place of all of us who had *never* worshiped God. Trust Jesus, and you'll be forgiven. You'll be remade from the inside out. You'll begin the life of worship that these psalms describe.

Let the gospel fuel your worship and extinguish your complaints.—Joe

"I began to weep loudly because no one was found worthy to open the scroll." — REVELATION 5:4

I don't cry very often (unlike Chris who gets teary-eyed over a thirty-second Hallmark commercial). I wish I cried more. When I look at the Scriptures, I see dozens of exemplary believers who cry. Joseph wept in compassion, Hannah in disappointment, David in sorrow, Nehemiah in heartache, Peter in repentance, Mary in grief, and the Lord Jesus Himself in bereavement and agony. Like I said, I wish I cried more. But I've experienced something strange as a pastor: when believers cry in my presence, they apologize for it almost every time. I tell them not to. I remind them that crying is the right response in so many situations. And I tell them that there's really only one kind of crying I'd bring to a stop: tears of inconsolable hopelessness.

In Revelation 5 John sees a vision of God seated on His throne holding a scroll. When John finds out that no one is able to take the parchment from God's hand, he starts crying (5:4). He doesn't just shed a few tears. He starts wailing! Is this just the overreaction of an emotionally unstable man? Not at all. John understands the symbolism. If no one in heaven or on earth is able to hold the scroll—the title deed to the universe—it appears there's no one who can rule the world, no one who can right the wrongs, no one who can still the chaos. You can totally understand why John was crying! His life was in apparent shambles at this point. When John received this vision, he himself was old and imprisoned; he had endured the beheading of his brother and the deaths of his closest associates; the churches in which he had invested his life were struggling with apathy, immorality, and persecution; and now, when he sees that the scroll is untouched—that there's no mediator to bring justice on earth—he begins to wail. Thankfully, as he grieved, one of the elders came from the throne and commanded John, "Stop weeping" (5:5, NASB). He then told him to behold the Conqueror.

Jesus is the Lion who stops our crying. There is one Person in the world worthy to bring judgment and salvation on earth. It's the mighty Lion from the kingly tribe of Judah; it's the one who is both the Root and Offshoot of King David (5:5). After He ascended into heaven, Jesus took hold of the scroll and "sat down at the right hand of the Majesty on high" (Hebrews 1:3). The Lion is sovereign, leading this messed-up world to His intended goal. So, believer, stop weeping tears of hopelessness.

Jesus is the Lamb we'll never stop praising. When John gazes toward the throne to catch a glimpse of the Lion, instead of seeing a lion, he sees a Lamb that appears to have been killed. The Lion is the Lamb. The symbolism is profound: the Lion who will conquer is the Lamb who was crushed. Whereas God the Father has authority over all of creation because He created it (4:11), the Lamb is given sovereign authority over creation because He was slain (5:9-10). There's a connection between Jesus' death for creation and His authority over it. Jesus can mediate divine judgment over all of creation because He Himself became a creature, because He submitted Himself to the curse of pain and death, because He died in the place of other sinful creatures to redeem them from sin and the curse, and because He was raised as Lord over the fallen creation. So, believer, the Lamb is the Lion. Don't be hopeless.

When John sees the Lamb, he stops crying, and all creation erupts with thunderous praise. Wailing gives way to worship. Why? Because getting a glimpse of Jesus as both the Lion and the Lamb is getting a glimpse of the naked glory of God. It's seeing, as Jonathan Edwards preached, "the admirable conjunction of diverse excellencies in Jesus Christ" ("The Excellency of Jesus Christ"). Here is the very glory of God! Jesus is God and man, Sovereign and Sacrifice, mighty and meek, slaughtered yet standing, humble yet highly exalted, the Lion and the Lamb.

Believer, never cry tears of inconsolable hopelessness. Not if Jesus holds the scroll. He redeemed you by His blood, He rose again from the dead, He reigns forevermore, and He's returning to earth as King over every king. Behold the Lion and the Lamb.

Let the gospel keep you from ever crying tears of inconsolable hopelessness.—Joe

"All this has come upon us, though we have not forgotten you." — PSALM 44:17

"I deserve better." That thought is the root of much discouragement. Yes, we have tough circumstances. But we also have *lofty expectations.* Even if we reject "The Prosperity Gospel" of T. D. Jakes and Joel Osteen (which cruelly creates false expectations), we still feel that obedience brings blessings.

We're not alone. The writer of Psalm 44 expressed the same frustrations. For the first eight verses, it seems that he's going to praise God for being Israel's champion in the past, specifically in their conquest of Canaan. He rightly attributes Israel's success not to their military prowess but to God's mighty arm (v. 3). He says that he too is trusting God, not his own abilities or devices (v. 6). Sounds like a happy psalm.

But in verse 9 he sets the hook, taking God to task. The rest of the psalm is a complaint that God has led Israel into *defeat* rather than victory! They've been disgraced (v. 9), defeated (v. 10), spoiled (v. 10), slaughtered (v. 11), scattered (v. 11), sold (v. 12), mocked (vv. 13-14), and demoralized (vv. 15-16). The worst part, in the psalmist's mind, is that *they didn't deserve it.* They hadn't been sinless, but they had been faithful (vs. idolatrous), just as their forefathers had. Yet, instead of redeeming them, God was selling them cheaply, as at a rummage sale. The psalmist expects triumph for God's sake. Instead, he laments that the Israelites were being *slaughtered* for God's sake (v. 22). *"Our faith—rather than gaining us blessings—is the very reason for our persecution. Our fidelity to You is getting us crushed!"*

Is the psalmist right? Absolutely! Sometimes obedience brings trouble. In fact, Paul is going to quote Psalm 44:22 in Romans 8:36, pointing out to suffering Christians that God's people have always been led like lambs to the slaughter. It's not a surprise (1 Peter 4:12-19). It's not a mistake. It's actually a privilege (Acts 5:41). And it's certainly not evidence that God doesn't love us. Indeed, Paul's affirmation in Romans 8:35 that nothing can separate us from the love of God focuses not on people but on problems: "Who shall separate us from the love of Christ? Shall tribulation, or distress, or persecution, or famine, or nakedness, or danger, or sword?" No! A thousand times no! Poverty, illness, bereavement, disappointment, persecution—these things don't mean that God doesn't love you. He loves you infinitely. But sometimes following Him will mean going with Him like a lamb to the slaughter:

> He was oppressed, and he was afflicted….Like a lamb that is led to the slaughter, and like a sheep that before its shearers is silent, so he opened not his mouth (Isaiah 53:7).

You serve a bloody Savior. You follow martyred disciples. You are part of a persecuted church. Change your expectations. Don't believe the lie that obedience will bring about what Osteen calls *Your Best Life Now.* Thank God that what we have now is as *bad* as it will ever get for those of us who have trusted Christ. Our "best life" is yet to come. "For I consider that the sufferings of this present time are not worth comparing with the glory that is to be revealed to us" (Romans 8:18).

Take heart from the gritty but grace-filled lessons of Psalm 44:
- Faithfulness doesn't always bring God's blessing. And suffering doesn't indicate God's displeasure with you. Divest yourself of those unbiblical and faith-quenching lies.
- You're allowed to pray angry. The psalmist—under inspiration, in a book that teaches us how to worship—shoots straight with God, complaining, arguing, even asking God to wake up. Since God inspired the psalm, apparently He's okay with that kind of transparency in prayer. If you're frustrated, or confused, or feeling forgotten, tell Him so!
- God will use His people for His glory. He may do so by blessing us, like the Israelites during the conquest. Or He may do so by sustaining us through affliction, like the Israelites at later times and like the church through the ages. Either way is fine (Philippians 1:20).
- Long for the best blessings of obedience: those which are eternal, and awaiting you.

Let the gospel assure you of God's love, even in your disappointments.—Chris

"Let us therefore draw near with confidence to the throne of grace." — HEBREWS 4:16

In February of 2013, I received that phone call that no one wants to get. It was my urologist: "Your biopsy has come back positive. You have cancer." My immediate reaction was to seek human consolation. But the comfort was minimal. I wanted someone to fix the problem and no one could. For about forty-eight hours I was on an emotional roller-coaster. But then something unexplainable happened. Suddenly I found myself able to cope. As time passed, people would tell me how amazed they were that I was handling my unsettling news so well. I had only one answer for them: "What you see and what I'm experiencing has to be none other than the sustaining grace of God." I mean, I am the quintessential worrier. When life spins out of control, anxiety tends to engulf me. But I was calm. I was experiencing the grace of God on a level I had never known. As I faced the prospect of surgery and the inevitable time of waiting that follows, God's grace was never in short supply.

All of us know that it is one thing to embrace the truth of Scripture theoretically, but it is altogether different to have that truth affirmed practically. You are no doubt familiar with the Lord's words to Paul in 2 Corinthians 12:9 where He affirms, "My grace is sufficient for you, for my power is made perfect in weakness." My weakness was a disease that was potentially lethal. Nor was it within my power to calm my fractured emotions. These words to Paul had become more than theory to me. What I was experiencing was God's sufficiency in action.

Beyond that, I knew this was God's sovereign plan for me, for He is the One "who works all things after the counsel of his will" (Ephesians 1:11). And so I rested in that truth and purposed to glorify Him whatever the outcome. Like Paul, I prepared myself to embrace God's will, "whether by life or by death" (Philippians 1:20). I was learning that "the grace in which we stand" (Romans 5:2) is the same grace that will sustain us until our journey is complete.

Since my diagnosis, the promise of God's faithfulness has likewise taken on a whole new meaning. As a Christian, I have always believed that "God is faithful" (1 Corinthians 1:9). At least I have always believed it in my head. But in my heart? Umm, not so much. There was often a subtle, nagging doubt that would not go away. Yet, I now found myself once again getting beyond the theoretical. It hit me like a thunderbolt. God's faithfulness became very real to me. God was faithful—to me! He was committed—to me! He was loyal—to me! No earthly friends had ever matched such a commitment, nor are they ever likely to do so. I learned that God's faithfulness was evident even in the affliction itself. The words of the psalmist brought uncommon comfort: "I know, O LORD, that your judgments are righteous, and that in faithfulness you have afflicted me" (Psalm 119:75). And let's be honest here; it sometimes takes God's grace to accept the fact that affliction is an act of His faithfulness.

Not too many years ago a good friend of mine and faithful servant of God passed away after battling Lou Gehrig's disease. Shortly after that, I learned that my dad had been diagnosed with esophageal cancer, from which he later died. In response to those circumstances, I penned the words to a song that expressed what I was feeling at the time. Writing this song was spiritually therapeutic and reassuring. The song continues to comfort me to this day.

> *Questions go unanswered and I long to understand,*
> *Yet I must believe that You are God, embrace Your sovereign plan.*
> *Before I was afflicted how my heart would go astray,*
> *But I've learned affliction is a friend that leads me to obey.*
>
> *Surrounded by disease and death, misfortune and despair,*
> *In my weakness and my unbelief, I question if You're there.*
> *But then I read the words of Job where he affirms to me:*
> *"Shall we accept the good from God and not adversity?"*
>
> *Now with trembling heart, O Lord, I'll trust what I can't see*
> *I'll walk the path that You've ordained wherever it may lead.*
> *And if affliction must be part of this my earthly race,*
> *Sustain me till the Night is past; uphold me with Your grace.*

Let the truth of the gospel bring you uncommon comfort and assurance.—Dan Totten

18 | Truth for Unstable Times

"The Most High rules the kingdom of men and gives it to whom he will." — DANIEL 4:25

I first taught the book of Daniel in September 2008, three days after President George W. Bush told the US that our economy was facing "unprecedented danger." Within two months, we had elected a new president. Within three months, the housing market collapsed. Within four months, ten percent of the members in our congregation were unemployed. The end of 2008 is a relatively small but vivid reminder that we are living—as all of God's people throughout history have lived—in a time of political and economic upheaval. Our lives are never as stable and secure as we'd like to imagine. The six historical accounts that are recorded in the first six chapters of Daniel have a single main point to help us deal with instability and insecurity.

Daniel 1. After being deported from Jerusalem to Babylon (605 BC) to serve in the king's court, Daniel and his friends refused to eat the king's choice foods. Yet they excelled physically, intellectually, and spiritually. At this point, Daniel was probably fifteen to twenty years old. What was God doing? One thing: Showing that His resources were superior to the king's.

Daniel 2. Nebuchadnezzar had a troubling dream and demanded that his magicians tell him both the dream and its interpretation—or perish (2:1-16). After praying to God (2:17-24), Daniel recounted and interpreted Nebuchadnezzar's dream of the great statue (2:25-45). The dream revealed that every great world power—Babylon, Medo-Persia, Greece, and Rome— would be overpowered by the kingdom of the Lord and His Messiah. The king affirmed to Daniel, "Your God is God of gods and Lord of kings" (2:47).

Daniel 3. Nebuchadnezzar made an idolatrous image (possibly like the one in his dream). Because Shadrach, Meshach, and Abednego refused to worship it (3:1-18), they were cast into a furnace of fire (3:19-23). The Babylonians saw in the furnace that these three were walking around with a fourth person who appeared to be divine (3:24-27). When the king witnessed this miracle, he said, "There is no other god who is able to rescue in this way" (3:29).

Daniel 4. Nebuchadnezzar recounted how he was utterly abased by the Most High God for his arrogance. He had a dream regarding a great tree being cut down (4:4-18) which foretold his approaching humiliation (4:19-27). Within a year, the mighty king was humbled by God just as Daniel had prophesied (4:28-33). King Nebuchadnezzar affirmed that God's "kingdom is an everlasting kingdom" (4:3, 34; memorize 4:35!).

Daniel 5. At a huge feast Belshazzar, Nebuchadnezzar's son, blasphemously drank from the vessels his father had taken from the temple in Jerusalem (5:1-4). Suddenly, he saw a hand writing on the wall (5:5-9). He called Daniel for an interpretation (5:10-16). Now around eighty years old, Daniel warned of God's impending judgment (5:17-28). He boldly told Belshazzar that "the Most High God" had given him his reign (5:18) and was now taking it (5:28).

Daniel 6. King Darius foolishly signed a self-aggrandizing religious decree (6:1-9) which Daniel—now over eighty years old—conscientiously disobeyed. Darius reluctantly sentenced Daniel to the lions' den (6:10-18). God protected Daniel throughout the night (6:19-23), leading Darius to proclaim: "The God of Daniel…is the living God, enduring forever; his kingdom shall never be destroyed, and his dominion shall be to the end" (6:26).

In every one of these six chapters, God worked a miracle in order to reveal to the earthly king that He is the Most High King. The God of Israel is *the* God, the only God, the God over all wanna-be gods, the King over every king. The book of Daniel teaches us to have strong confidence in the Lord during times of international upheaval. When the Babylonians took over Jerusalem, God was in control. When the Medes conquered the Babylonians, God was in control. The same is true in our day: when nation rises against nation, God is in control. "Those [governing authorities] that exist have been instituted by God" (Romans 13:1). That truth isn't easy to digest, but it's absolutely biblical. Even though many people sin against God, no one thwarts His sovereign purposes. Not only does God reign presently, but He's *coming* to reign. God has ordained that all of human history will climax when the Son of Man establishes His political rule on the earth (Revelation 11:15). You can be confident that there's coming a day when this unstable, insecure world will be united under one Ruler. The skies could split today; it could happen in a few years or in a thousand, but it *will* happen (Daniel 2:44).

Let the gospel stabilize you during times of political insecurity.—Joe

"Be steadfast, immovable, always abounding in the work of the Lord."— 1 CORINTHIANS 15:58

In 1 Corinthians Paul addresses a laundry list of problems—arrogance and church divisions (chs. 1-4), wrong views of tolerance (chs. 5-6), errant views on sexuality (chs. 6-7), selfish views of Christian liberty (chs. 8-11), and worship services doing more harm than good (chs. 11-14). In chapter 15 Paul deals with yet another problem: some in the church were denying that Christians would experience a bodily resurrection. Paul confronts this error directly, and his answer provides remarkable comfort for exhausted believers.

Remember the gospel (vv.1-11). At the heart of the gospel are four monumental facts: Jesus' death and accompanying burial, and Jesus' resurrection and accompanying appearances. The burial proves He was really dead, and the appearances prove He was really alive. In order to be changed by this gospel, you must receive it, stand in it, and hold fast to it (15:1-2).

Consider the logic (vv. 12-19). Paul poses seven hypothetical consequences if Jesus hadn't risen. If the resurrection never happened, Paul's preaching is bogus, the faith of Christians is worthless, our loved ones who have died are gone forever, and we should be pitied as imbeciles (15:13-19). Even though the Christians in Corinth weren't directly questioning *Jesus'* resurrection, Paul shows how they were indirectly denying it. He says, in effect, "If you can't believe the general rule that God will raise the dead, then that would have to apply to Christ, too" (15:16).

Think theologically (vv. 20-34). Jesus was raised from the dead as the firstfruits. His resurrection shows not only that the harvest is coming but that it's already started. Paul's teaching regarding the first Adam and the last Adam is very similar to what he writes in Romans 5. There he argued, "If you're in Adam, you're condemned; if you're in Christ, you're justified." Here he says, "If you're in Adam, you die; if you're in Christ, you get raised." The big question for every human is this: "Are you in Adam or in Christ?"

Get some practical answers (vv. 35-49). The Corinthians questioned how the resurrection would happen and what kind of body would be raised. Paul gives simple answers: If God knows how to create all kinds of physical things—including people, birds, fish, and stars—then a resurrection body isn't all that hard for Him.

Understand new revelation (vs. 50-58). Paul reveals a mystery, something God had not previously revealed with this much clarity. In the previous section, he answered the question *how*; here he answers the question *when*. For believers, physical death is not the end. When Jesus returns, death will be conquered, and we will be raised instantaneously from the dead and given resurrection bodies. This is the very moment of which Isaiah prophesied: "The Lord will swallow up death for all time" (Isaiah 25:8), the moment when Jesus removes the terrifying fierceness of death. (Notice how Hosea 13:14 is turned on its head!)

Most of this chapter is straight talk about hard facts—facts to which every person must respond. You must believe the resurrection, especially in view of the empty tomb, the five hundred witnesses, and the disciples' changed lives and risky boldness, including Paul's! Once you believe these truths, Christian, you must live them out. Pursue holiness in your body. There's more to holiness than physical health, but eating, exercising, having sex, working, and sleeping should all be done to the glory of God because what you do in your body matters.

The final verse of the chapter (a great theme verse for life) challenges you to be strong and endure ministry hardships because of the resurrection. Notice the words *work* and *labor*. Paul says, "Abound in work for the Lord that's exhausting, toilsome, and physically draining." The Christian life right now is dominated by toil. Christ never promised ease. Fighting sin is hard work. Praying is hard work. Loving your spouse is hard work. Raising children for Christ is hard work. Providing for your family is hard work. Caring for your aging parents is hard work. Getting to church consistently is hard work. Serving in children's ministry is hard work. Forbearing with annoying Christians is hard work. How easy it would be to give up fighting, to cease being committed to the church, to let your children do as they please. A comfort-driven life would be fine if we didn't have the hope of resurrection. But Jesus has been raised, and we will be, too. So remain committed to a life of toil for Christ. It will be worth it all.

Let the gospel lead you to embrace exhausting toil for Jesus' sake.—Joe

"The Spirit himself intercedes for us with groanings too deep for words." — ROMANS 8:26

Can God suffer? Can He sorrow? Is sorrow a *human* emotion, or a reflection of *God's image* in man? It's a complicated question. The doctrine usually called the "impassibility of God" teaches that God is so transcendent that He never suffers. It helpfully prevents us from thinking of God as needy, susceptible, and passive. A sovereign God cannot be injured, surprised, or harmed. God is never victimized. God is never at a loss. But can He *feel*? Can He *grieve*? I believe that the answer is yes, and I find His empathetic sorrow immensely comforting.

Scripture teaches that God the Father grieves with His people. The Old Testament Scriptures speak of God being "sorry" and "grieved to his heart" about man's sinfulness (Genesis 6:6-7). He was moved by the mistreatment of His people (Exodus 2:23-25; Judges 10:16). His heart hurt and yearned for His oppressed people (Jeremiah 31:20; Isaiah 49:15; Hosea 11:8). He has no delight in the death of the wicked—which must mean that He instead is saddened by it (Ezekiel 18:23; 33:11). Some argue that OT descriptions of God's sorrow are merely anthropomorphisms (or more accurately, anthropopathisms—attributing to God our human feelings, to aid our understanding). I suggest that the exact *opposite* is true. We are created in God's image, and our emotions are reflections of *His*. God is compassionate, merciful, and loving. He feels holy joy, holy wrath, and holy hatred. It is reasonable that He feels holy sorrow, even in the millennia prior to Christ's birth. D. A. Carson agrees:

> The biblical evidence, in both Testaments, pictures God as a being who can suffer. Doubtless God's suffering is not exactly like ours; doubtless metaphors litter the descriptions. But... they are metaphors that refer to God and are suggestive of his profound emotional life and his distinctly personal relationship with his people (*How Long, O Lord*, pp. 187-88).

Scripture teaches that God the Son grieves with His people. This is the part of the discussion that is easy. We know that Jesus hungered, thirsted, and bled. Those are uniquely human experiences. But He also wept. Was that a part of His perfect humanity, or was it part of His revelation of the invisible God (John 1:18; 14:9)? I believe that in Christ's sorrow we see the heart of God. To see Christ weep over a funeral service (John 11:30) or a massive crowd (Matthew 9:35-38) or a wicked city (Luke 19:41-44) is to see God weep. Jesus sorrowed while on earth, but He suffers with us still. For example, He says that Saul is persecuting *Him* by persecuting the church (Acts 9:4-5). Jesus feels our pain (Hebrews 4:15-16). When we suffer, Christ suffers with us. Does this knowledge not make pain more bearable?

Scripture teaches that God the Spirit grieves with His people. The Holy Spirit is a person who thinks, acts, and feels, perfectly. In a tender passage in Romans 8:18-27, we read that creation groans under the curse (v. 22). Christians groan as well (v. 23). Amazingly, the Spirit groans out prayers for us, empathizing with our grief and translating our sighs into requests to God. Further, the Spirit is grieved by our sin (Ephesians 4:30). And it is the Spirit who produces virtue in us whereby we both rejoice with the joyful and weep with the grieving (Romans 12:12). The Spirit feels our loss and groans. What grace!

John Stott relates how central the idea of a suffering, empathizing God was to his own faith:

> I could never myself believe in God, if it were not for the cross....In the real world of pain, how could one worship a God who was immune to it. I have entered many Buddhist temples in different Asian countries and stood respectfully before the statue of the Buddha, his legs crossed, arms folded, eyes closed, the ghost of a smile playing round his mouth, a remote look on his face, detached from the agonies of the world. But each time after a while I have had to turn away. And in imagination I have turned instead to that lonely, twisted, tortured figure on the cross, nails through hands and feet, back lacerated, limbs wrenched, brow bleeding from thorn-pricks, mouth dry and intolerably thirsty, plunged in God-forsaken darkness. That is the God for me! He laid aside his immunity to pain. He entered our world of flesh and blood, tears and death. He suffered for us. Our sufferings become more manageable in the light of his (*The Cross of Christ*, pp. 326-27).

Let the gospel remind you that the Father, Son, and Spirit are touched with your grief.—Chris

"The promise of entering his rest still stands." — HEBREWS 4:1

You're in a war. Faith is your most crucial piece of armor, and unbelief is your greatest weakness. Hebrews 3:7-4:13 is an inspired sermon on Psalm 95:7b-11, a Davidic song that remembered Israel's unbelief in the days of Moses (Numbers 14:28-30). After the twelve spies returned from scouting out the Promised Land, Israel decided not to obey the Lord's command to possess Canaan. God judged the entire nation with forty years of wilderness wandering, and He forbade them from "entering His rest." The writer to the Hebrews uses this history to warn the suffering believers of unbelief (Hebrews 3:7-19) and the resulting eternal consequence (Hebrews 4:1-13). He takes pains to prove, based on Psalm 95:11, that God's rest didn't simply refer to the promised land of Canaan and that people today can still either enter God's eternal rest by faith or fail to enter it through unbelief.

Christian, you need to beware of falling away! If this message was appropriate for Jewish Christians in first-century Rome, it's appropriate for you. Does it sound odd to you that God is warning believers about falling away? It may seem strange if you believe in eternal security (like I do), but you dare not brush off God's Word when He warns you about falling away. The Scriptures clearly teach both that God will preserve true believers until the day they see Christ (Philippians 1:6; Romans 8:28-30; Jude 24) and that true believers will persevere in their faith (Matthew 10:22; Hebrews 3:6, 14; Colossians 1:23; John 15:1-6; 1 John 2:24). By God's grace true believers endure, hold on, and remain. However, beware if your view of eternal security leads to spiritual complacency. How dangerous! Genuine Christians live with both a fear that they could fall back into their old lifestyle and a confidence that God will never let them. God keeps true believers, but God Himself warns them against falling away. Don't take the teeth out of the passage! The writer offers at least four habits that fuel perseverance.

Experience daily encouragement in Jesus' church. God commands His people to speak words of encouragement and loving correction to each other daily (3:13). You need other believers, and other believers need you. God designed the church to aid in the perseverance of believers. He wants the church to be a source of daily—not just weekly—encouragement. With that in mind, do you have relationships with at least a few other believers whereby you can be encouraged as you transparently share your weaknesses, doubts, temptations, and burdens?

Meditate on the rest you've found in Jesus. Hebrews 4:1-11 ties together thousands of years of biblical teaching on rest—from the *beginning* of rest at Creation, to the *reminder* of God's rest in the Ten Commandments, to the *illustration* of rest in the conquest of Canaan, to the *fulfillment* of rest in being saved through faith in Christ, to the *perfection* of rest in the Holy City. You'll find strength to persevere as you meditate on the rest you found when you first looked to Jesus and on the rest you'll find when you finally see Him with your very eyes.

Continually expose yourself to God's living, piercing Word. After considering Psalm 95, the author exclaims, "Do you see how alive and how powerful Psalm 95 is! It meets you in your trial, alters your values, makes you fear what you should fear, challenges your small compromises, exposes your self-centered motives, entices you to pursue God's rest, and carves the deception of sin" (see 4:12-13). Believer, digest God's word regularly. It will keep you from falling.

Draw near to Jesus' throne of grace. "Come boldly unto the throne of grace, that [you] may obtain mercy, and find grace to help in time of need" (4:16, KJV). Is there a more beautiful, more compelling invitation to prayer in all of the Bible? Your sympathetic, enthroned High Priest urges you to boldly approach Him. In prayer you'll find strength to keep fighting.

Your perseverance will be tested in trial after trial after trial. You'll be mocked by family and friends, abused by false teachers, disappointed by other Christians, haunted by besetting sins, riddled with recurring physical sufferings, enticed ten thousand times to live for this present world, and continually discouraged by unrelenting stress. If you're a true Christian, you'll persevere through it all. Even though you'll come out of the war limping with many regrets and scars, you'll come through. It might have been easier to stop fighting, but true believers can't. We have faith that perseveres. In the Christian war, there's only one thing that you should really fear: letting go of Jesus.

Let the gospel fuel your perseverance.—Joe

"O Lord, behold my affliction." — LAMENTATIONS 1:9

Lamentations has a few well-known verses, but it's not a popular book! How many times have you been to a Bible study on Lamentations? How often have you heard a series of sermons through it? As the title suggests, these five chapters are cries of anguish over God's horrific judgments on Jerusalem. Jeremiah pleads for the Lord to give attention to Jerusalem's miserable condition: she's like a desolate widow, a princess-turned-slave, a rejected prostitute (ch. 1). He weeps over what the Lord has done to Jerusalem in His anger (ch. 2), yet Jeremiah remains certain of God's unfailing love (ch. 3). As the pitiful song continues, the "weeping prophet" surveys the city's shameful condition (ch. 4), then again begs the Lord to look at the reproach of Jerusalem (ch. 5). In his final plea Jeremiah essentially cries, "Lord, we have no inheritance, no security, no freedom, no food, no dignity, no joy, and no strength. O King, restore us, unless You've totally rejected us" (see especially 5:19-22). No wonder the book's not popular! It's focused on the dreadful experience of God's judgment, and it ends with dissonance.

But it's a valuable book, especially for the hurting. Most English speakers are unaware that the first four chapters of Lamentations are tightly constructed acrostic poems. Barry Webb observes, "It is somewhat startling to discover that a book that portrays such radical disorientation should be one of the most ordered works in the Old Testament" (*Five Festal Garments*, p. 60). Hurting believer, you have much to learn from the "controlled venting" of Lamentations. It teaches you to channel your grief in five ways.

Lament your experience of sin's judgment. You live in a broken world. Death, tears, pain, disease, sweat, and natural disasters are all results of the Fall. If you're a Christian, all such judgments are not condemnatory, and they are only temporary. Yet, you still experience them, and they still hurt. Let Jeremiah's lamentations be a model for you: a godly believer—one who's experiencing God's judgment—laments.

Grieve when God's judgment falls on others. Christians can be prone to a "they-had-it-coming" mentality when they watch God's judgment fall on others. Even when distress may truly be what they deserve, let Jeremiah teach you to grieve when others experience God's judgment.

Hate the sin that requires God's judgment. Read Lamentations and make a list of the sins of Jerusalem and of the judgments she experienced for those sins. They're intertwined. Israel cried, "My transgressions were bound into a yoke; by his hand they were fastened together; they were set upon my neck" (1:14). The terrible judgment highlighted how terrible the sin was that caused it to fall. Sin is horrific, especially the sin of idolatry. Believer, as you experience hardships in life, don't turn toward the idolatrous comfort of pleasure, possessions, or the praise of men. Such spiritual adultery brought about all the hardships we endure today. Hate every enticement that draws you away from exclusive devotion to the Lord.

Fear the Lord who judges and saves. Lamentations reveals a God not to be toyed with. He "gives full vent to his wrath," and He "pour[s] out his hot anger" on people, cities, and civilizations (4:11). On the other hand, when He commits Himself to someone in love, He is forever faithful to that commitment. His faithfulness will never cease (3:22-23). The Lord is an eternal rock; He's a consuming fire. He's worthy of your dread and worthy of your devotion.

Thank Jesus for enduring God's judgment in your place. The heart of Jeremiah's poem expresses hope in God's faithfulness to His covenant promises (3:21-32). How does that work? How can a God committed to judging sin show committed love to sinners? In Jeremiah's day a crystal clear answer to these questions awaited the New Testament. The two chords didn't ultimately harmonize until God caused the judgment for all His people's iniquities to fall on His Son (Romans 3:21-26). So, each of Jeremiah's vivid descriptions of the pain of God's judgment should be a faint illustration of the unimaginable pain that the Messiah endured when He was made to be sin for your sake (2 Corinthians 5:21).

Let the gospel help you to express and control your emotions as you endure hardship.—Joe

"I have no greater joy than to hear that my children are walking in the truth." — 3 JOHN 4

If there is no greater joy than having children who walk in the truth, then there must be no greater sorrow than having children who don't. Rebelling children cause regretting parents (Proverbs 17:25). I've counseled scores of parents who are overcome by grief and guilt because of a wayward child. If you're a parent of a prodigal, there's no escape for your *grief*. Your grief is proof of your love. But there is escape for your *guilt*, whether it's justified or not.

For many, their shame is the result of bad doctrine they've imbibed from parenting gurus. Many books present fail-proof strategies for rearing perfect kids. Listen to Richard Fugate:

> Training children is not a hit-or-miss proposition in which the parent has no control. It is not that some children just turn out okay while others may not. There is no such thing as a bad seed….[Scripture offers] a promise from God that our children will turn out okay if we properly train them…a guarantee (*What the Bible Says about Parenting*, pp. 19, 21).

So my kids will be perfect—if I'm perfect. No pressure. Of course, that's not true. If their character and eternity rest solely on my performance, they have no chance. Frankly, there's no such thing as "good seed." My sinful children need Christ. I'm only part of the equation.

You will influence your child. I don't want to minimize the importance of wise parenting. Parents must obey biblical instructions, teaching their children the Scriptures and praying for their children to know and love Christ. Most importantly, parents must model what a humble, growing Christian looks like. Winning their love and respect will help win their souls (Proverbs 23:26; Ephesians 6:4). But you're not enough. You can't do it. Parents who think they can are generally proud of their "perfect kids"…for about eighteen years. Then the behavioristic lessons that focused on conformity rather than gospel-driven change start unraveling. The seemingly perfect kids can't get away fast enough, and the results are devastating for the entire family.

Your child's own choices will influence your child. Your child will be accountable for himself. Isn't that the whole point of the book of Proverbs, where a loving father urges his son to learn gospel-rooted wisdom about life and *hopes* he'll internalize the lessons? Isn't that the point of the fifth commandment, which commands children to obey with the very real potential that they *won't*? As Ted Tripp writes, "Children are never passive receivers of shaping. They are, rather, active responders" (*Shepherding a Child's Heart*, p. 32). There are plenty of parents in Scripture who had both obedient and disobedient children. Adam and Eve raised wicked Cain and righteous Abel. Isaac and Rebekah raised believing Jacob (a spiritual late-bloomer, to be sure) and carnal Esau. Jacob in turn raised both the conscientious Joseph (who fled from Potiphar's wife) and the adulterous Judah (who got his daughter-in-law pregnant, mistaking her for a prostitute). Mary and Joseph raised Jesus and a bunch of skeptics who didn't believe in Jesus for three decades. The point of these examples? Parents' faithfulness can't be entirely judged by the character of their children. Mercy, the fact that our Heavenly Father has children like *us* should be enough to debunk that guilt-inducing myth!

Ultimately, your child needs God. Many parenting plans fail to recognize that no parent can guarantee a child's salvation. Salvation is of the Lord, not mom and pop (Jonah 2:9b). We need divine intervention. That's the point of Psalm 127:1-2. Yes, train your children. Build their character. Protect them. But if God isn't working, your labor is in vain. Be *diligent* to do what you ought, then be *dependent* on God to do what you can't. "Build…Watch…Sleep."

You have regrets over your parenting. Who doesn't? You could have done better. But even if you had, you'd still be dependent on God's grace. Instead of succumbing to Satan's vicious accusations, look to Christ. Pray for grace for your wayward child. Rejoice that God loves your child more than you do, and He can actually change the prodigal's heart. If the four Gospels tell us anything, it's that Jesus has a soft spot for the prayers of parents. And while you're pleading for grace, go ahead and apply it to yourself, too. You're not perfect. You sin. You may need to repent of being a harsh, or aloof, or doting parent. Ask God to forgive you. Humbly ask your *kids* to forgive you. Owning your failures may soften their hearts. But then stop beating yourself up. Rejoice that God has grace to cover *your* waywardness, too.

Let the gospel soothe your conscience over the past and give you hope for the future.—Chris

"Be strong and courageous. Do not be frightened, and do not be dismayed, for the LORD your God is with you wherever you go." — JOSHUA 1:9

God never gives His people an assignment without also giving them the necessary resources for accomplishing it. As Carolyn Hamlin beautifully wrote, "His will cannot lead you where His grace will not keep you." God's calling always comes with His enabling power. In these first verses of Joshua, the Lord commissions Israel's new leader, giving Joshua a daunting task. Then God reassures him that he'll have all he needs for certain success.

God's calling Joshua to lead Israel in its conquest of the promised land was intimidating because of three massive obstacles. First, God's people had just lost a great leader. Imagine Israel hearing the news, "Moses is dead" (1:2). Imagine *Joshua* hearing it. Throughout his forty years of service Moses had proved to be the greatest leader Israel had in its first 1,000 years of existence (Deuteronomy 34:10). How would you like to be Joshua, trying to follow Moses? The second obstacle Joshua faced was the promised land. God's people had a massive task in front of them. To get an idea of the size of this undertaking, you need to get out a map and chart the locations in Joshua 1:4, then you need to read chapters 12-21. You're not only dealing with a massive piece of real estate but also with numerous hostile people groups. Israel had to conquer several hundred cities. I counted 115 cities for the tribe of Judah alone (Joshua 15). This was a huge job—one Joshua could only begin to see accomplished. After twenty years of leading the conquest, aged Joshua had to tell the nation to keep driving the people out (Joshua 23). The third obstacle Joshua faced was the nation of Israel herself. God commanded, "Go over this Jordan, you and all this people" (1:2). Think of *all this people.* Think of the past forty years in the wilderness. Think of their fickleness, their idolatry at Sinai, their unbelief at Kadesh-barnea, their rebellion against God's leader Moses, and their constant complaining. Those were the people that Joshua was asked to lead. How exciting! I would guess that every Christian can relate to Joshua's fear. Like him, you sense that God's call on your life—to rear your children in Jesus' nurture, to rejoice in all your trials, to love those who offend you, to fight and conquer the sins that so easily beset you, to speak the gospel—is way beyond your ability. I mean, look at you, look at your past, look at your fellow believers. How can you be strong and courageous?

As Joshua faced these intimidating obstacles, God gave him three comforting reassurances. First, God reminded Joshua of His *promise* (vv. 3-4). "I have given you this land, just as I promised to Moses." But Moses wasn't the first to receive this promise. The promise was six centuries old! It was first given to Abraham (Genesis 12:1-9). God was going to make good on this promise. Joshua needed to believe it, then act on it. Second, God assured Joshua of His *presence* (vv. 5-6). The Lord said, "Just as I was with Moses, so I will be with you. I will not leave you or forsake you." Third, God gave Joshua His *Law* (vv. 7-8). He said, "[This is the Law] that Moses my servant commanded you" (v. 7). Already in Joshua's day, Moses' words were in a book and were recognized as having God's own authority. Joshua was to keep the first five books of the Bible (all he had at the time) constantly in front of him. God wanted Joshua to speak God's Word, meditate on it, and carefully obey it. In giving Joshua His promise, His presence, and His Law, God had given Joshua every resource he would need. These resources are deeply interconnected: God's promises are revealed in His Word, and God's presence is one of His most consistent promises. So, meditation on God's Word would constantly assure Joshua of God's promised presence.

Christian, you too have God's promises, presence, and sufficient Word. In Jesus Christ all God's promises find their assured fulfillment (2 Corinthians 1:20)! Those who are in Jesus are assured of God's unfailing presence. "I will never leave or forsake you" was a promise not only for Joshua but for every Christian (Hebrews 13:5-6). Further, Christians have the sufficient Scriptures which point to Jesus (2 Timothy 3:14 – 4:5). So, if you have Christ, you have all the resources you need to live out God's calling on your life. You don't need to be "frightened or dismayed" as you face the overwhelming trials God has called you to face. Like Joshua you can "be strong and courageous."

Let the gospel inspire your courageous outlook.—Joe

"Why are you cast down, O my soul, and why are you in turmoil within me? Hope in God."
— PSALM 42:5

In his book *Spiritual Depression*, D. Martin Lloyd Jones, the insightful pastor of London's Westminster Chapel from 1939 through 1968, warned that too many Christians listen to themselves rather than talking to themselves. "The main art of spiritual living is to know how to handle yourself. You have to take yourself in hand, you have to address yourself, preach to yourself, question yourself" (*Spiritual Depression*, p. 21). We too often allow our thoughts to run astray rather than corralling and controlling them through biblical meditation. Especially when we're discouraged—"cast down," to use the language of Psalms 42-43—we need to talk ourselves out of our depression.

Notice first the structure of this pair of Psalms (which should be read as a single unit). They take us through three stanzas of complaint, each of which results in the thrice-repeated refrain: "Why are you cast down, O my soul, and why are you in turmoil within me? Hope in God; for I shall again praise him, my salvation and my God" (Psalm 42:5, 11; 43:5).

In the first stanza (42:1-4), the psalmist expresses his desperate longing for God (42:1). His "deer-like" thirst expresses not a worshiper's love for God (as we often think of the phrase) but the agonizing, terrifying thirst of an animal wasting away in a time of drought. The psalmist is beside himself with grief. He is oppressed. He has been exiled from Jerusalem and the temple, far away to the northern border of Israel (the locations of Mounts Hermon and Mizar in 42:6). Away from the temple, he feels exiled from God Himself (42:2). He feasts only on tears, day and night (42:3a). He is tormented by enemies who mock him by mocking His God (42:3b). From afar, he remembers the times of corporate worship when he led the people of Israel in praise (42:4). (Note: The authors, the sons of Korah, were temple musicians). However, even that glorious memory is bittersweet, for it reminds him of all that he's lost. Finally, he talks to himself: "What's wrong with you? Why are you giving up? Why are you depressed? Hope in God" (42:5)!

So did the darkness break? Depression rarely works that way. The psalmist admirably climbed out of his pit—*for a while*. Then the darkness returned. He admits as much at the start of the second stanza: "My soul is cast down...again" (42:6). He notes the irony of his request (he thirsts for "flowing streams," 42:1) with his present condition (he is being pummeled by depths, "waterfalls," "breakers," and "waves," 42:7). His honesty is liberating. Apparently it's okay to look to God and say, "I'm drowning here. You're killing me." He rallies his faith and reminds himself of God's love (42:8). But immediately he is hit by yet another wave of doubt: "God, if You're my Rock, why does it feel like You've forgotten me? Why are You letting my oppressors win, even as I mourn? Where are You? They're taunting me—and You! They're asking where You are, and I'm wondering the same thing" (42:9-10). Once again, the psalmist stops listening to himself and starts talking: "What's wrong with you? Hope in God" (42:11)!

Does he live happily ever after? Hardly. In the third stanza (Psalm 43), he's still troubled. He calls out to God for vindication (43:1). Once again, he complains that whereas he runs to God for refuge from his assailants, he receives only rejection (43:2, compare 42:9). He asks God for light to dispel his darkness and for truth to correct his thinking—two great requests (43:3)! He asks that he might be restored to God's presence, both literally (by returning to the temple) and spiritually (by a repairing of broken fellowship). The result of such grace will not only be his comfort but God's great glory (43:4). This is a wise prayer: "God, rescue me, that I may worship You." For a third time, after cycling through faith and doubt, the psalmist talks to himself. "What's wrong with you? Hope in God" (43:11).

Fighting your way out of John Bunyan's "slough of despond" (or the *Princess Bride's* "pit of despair") isn't easy. You don't just quote a verse, say a prayer, and triumph. But don't give up. Be encouraged that the sons of Korah—under divine inspiration!—recorded the same ups and downs, the same inconsistency, the same desperation. And they prayed, with success, to the same God and Savior. How much more can you, knowing of the finished work of Christ, preach yourself through depression! Grace!

Let the gospel inspire you to fight for joy—again and again and again.—Chris

"Moreover, I saw under the sun that…in the place of righteousness, even there was wickedness."
— ECCLESIASTES 3:16

One of our problems when we study the Bible is that we miss the forest for the trees. Why? It may be that Christians don't read the Bible fast enough. We study verses (trees) without studying books (forests). Good Bible study balances both big-picture and tiny-detail examination.

Think about three wisdom books: Proverbs, Job, and Ecclesiastes. What's the main point of each? Simply put, each book teaches you to fear the Lord (Proverbs 1:7; Job 28:28; Ecclesiastes 12:13). Proverbs teaches you that fearing God means humbly obeying His commands. If you want a blessed and successful life, you must choose to heed God's counsel and reject the enticements of fools. Job teaches you that fearing God means humbly trusting His will when you don't have a clue what He's doing. If you want comfort in your suffering, you must fear your Sovereign and be content not to know mysteries which He hasn't revealed. Ecclesiastes teaches you that fearing God means humbly enjoying the life He's given you even as many things about life frustrate you. If you want "the good life," you must be satisfied when there is no explanation for life's perplexities and inequities.

Each of these books is teaching the same kind of life, but they come at it from different angles. I love Derek Kidner's vivid illustration of the books' themes:

> If one had to design a cover for each of [these] books, drawn from their own contents, one might represent them by the various houses they describe. For Proverbs it could appropriately be the sevenpillared house of Wisdom….For Job, a very different picture: perhaps the wreckage in which his family perished when 'a great wind came across the wilderness and struck the four corners of the house'….As for Ecclesiastes, its insistence on the transience of earthly glory could hardly find a better symbol than its own description of a great house (12:3-4) in the grip of slow, inexorable decay (*The Wisdom of Proverbs, Job, and Ecclesiastes*, p. 116).

So Proverbs is like a beautiful Southern plantation, Job like a collapsed pile of lumber after a tornado has passed through, and Ecclesiastes like a cobweb-infested and structurally unsafe mansion that hasn't been lived in for a few centuries. Yet every house has the same welcome plaque on the front door: "Fear the Lord." These three books reinforce and complement each other. In other words, Proverbs is absolutely true, Job is absolutely true, and Ecclesiastes is absolutely true, but they must be understood *together*! They must be read in stereo. To try to understand Proverbs apart from Job will make you one of Job's friends. To understand Ecclesiastes without Proverbs will make you a disillusioned cynic. Proverbs teaches God's way to blessing, Job teaches that serving God doesn't necessarily lead to blessing, and Ecclesiastes teaches that God's blessings are not to be sought as gods. And all are true!

Does this "forest perspective" have any practical application to real life? Absolutely. In fact, it applies to every area of life. Consider what each book says about marriage. Proverbs teaches that marriage can be sweet or horrid depending on the character of the individuals involved (see, for example, Proverbs 12:4). Job, however, teaches that marriage is sometimes really tough for those who fear the Lord (Job 2:9-10). Ecclesiastes teaches that the joys of marriage are short-lived (Ecclesiastes 9:9). If you focus only on how to ensure a healthy marriage, yet receive relatively little teaching on the struggles and vanity of marriage, you'll not cope well with real life. You don't just need marriage advice. You need to know how to trust God when your wife dies or how to live for God even when you "do everything right" and your husband doesn't change. You need to live out all three wisdom books!

Your Savior lived out all three. Jesus perfectly followed Solomon's sage advice, walking in the way of wisdom and avoiding the path of folly. Yet, even worse than Job, this God-fearer experienced undeserved testing. And, like the wise Preacher counseled a millennium before, Jesus feared God even when justice seemed to be turned on its head, when wicked men sentenced Him to death, and when your wickedness was imputed to Him. Through it all, Jesus feared the Lord. Christian, follow your Savior's real-world wisdom: Fear the Lord when it leads to blessing, when it leads to testing, and when you can't see what difference your godliness makes.

Let the gospel teach you to fear the Lord, especially when life doesn't make sense.—Joe

"Jesus, Son of David, have mercy on me!" — LUKE 18:38

On July 6, 1415, John Huss was tied to a stake and surrounded by wood and straw. As rector of the University of Prague, he had been influenced by John Wycliffe's evangelical teaching and would in turn be a forerunner of the reformers of the following century and of the missionary-minded Moravians. However, his gospel preaching earned him only condemnation as a heretic. Asked by the Roman Catholic Council of Constance to recant of his errors, the undaunted Huss replied as follows:

> What errors shall I renounce? I know myself guilty of none. I call God to witness that all that I have written and preached has been with the view of rescuing souls from sin and perdition; and, therefore, most joyfully will I confirm with my blood that truth which I have written and preached.

As the pyre was lit, Huss met the flames with a song. His dying prayer was a quotation of Luke 18:38: "Jesus, thou Son of David, have mercy on me!" Mankind had no mercy. The Lord Jesus certainly did, welcoming the valiant gospel preacher to paradise.

Huss's final words were a repetition of a request by a blind man in Jericho. The blind man's cry for help was met with rebuke from pitiless men (v. 39a). Undeterred by those who would hush him, he cried out all the more: "Son of David, have mercy on me" (v. 39b). Our Lord—whose compassion is magnified in juxtaposition to the crowd's harshness—stopped, listened to the man, and granted his request for sight (vv. 41-42). Imagine the scene as the man uses his remade eyes to look on and follow Christ; hear him glorifying God; see the crowd as it shifts from criticism to praise (v. 43). And learn this lesson well: our Savior *delights* in mercy.

I suggest that you add that prayer to your repertoire. Memorize it. Meditate on it. Repeat it often, and urgently, and thoughtfully: *"Jesus, Son of David, have mercy on me."* When you're weary, ask for mercy. When you're suffocating under life's pressures, ask for mercy. When you're tempted to sin, ask for mercy. When you've fallen into sin again, for the umpteenth time, ask for mercy.

Know that you are praying to Jesus, who Himself is a man of sorrows who is acquainted with grief (Isaiah 53:3). Know that, further, He has borne *your* griefs and carried *your* sorrows (Isaiah 53:4). Know that He wept for the rebellious and the bereaved (Luke 19:41-44; John 11:33-35). Know that He is so gentle that He doesn't break a bruised reed or quench a smoldering wick (Matthew 12:20, quoting Isaiah 42:3). Know that He is gentle and lowly in heart (Matthew 11:29). Know that He has suffered temptation Himself and thus can sympathize with your weaknesses, responding to your cries for help with mercy and grace (Hebrews 2:18; 4:15-16).

In every distress, I have no better counsel for the hurting than this: run to Christ.

> *I run to Christ when chased by fear and find a refuge sure.*
> *"Believe in me," His voice I hear; His words and wounds secure.*
>
> *I run to Christ when torn by grief and find abundant peace.*
> *"I too had tears," He gently speaks; thus joy and sorrow meet.*
>
> *I run to Christ when worn by life and find my soul refreshed.*
> *"Come unto Me," He calls through strife; fatigue gives way to rest.*
>
> *I run to Christ when vexed by hell and find a mighty arm.*
> *"The Devil flees," the Scriptures tell; he roars, but cannot harm.*
>
> *I run to Christ when stalked by sin and find a sure escape.*
> *"Deliver me," I cry to Him; temptation yields to grace.*
>
> *I run to Christ when plagued by shame and find my one defense.*
> *"I bore God's wrath," He pleads my case—my Advocate and Friend.*

Let the gospel embolden you to cry out to Jesus the Son of David for mercy.—Chris

"Grace be with all who love our Lord Jesus Christ with love incorruptible." — EPHESIANS 6:24

Many Christians are uncomfortable with benedictions, assuming that they're only prayed by formal, lifeless congregations. If that's how you think, let me urge you not to throw the baby out with the bathwater! The fact that some gospel-less churches still use benedictions doesn't make the benedictions wrong. Benedictions are biblical. In fact, they're *Bible*. They open and close almost every letter in the New Testament. Paul ends his letter to the church at Ephesus praying for God to continually pour out His grace on those who love Jesus.

True Christians love Jesus, period. When Paul prays for God's grace to be given to all those who love Jesus with an undying love, it's another way of saying, "Grace be with every Christian." Christians are those who love Jesus, a Man who is both Lord and Christ. As Charles Hodge said, "Recognizing Christ as Jehovah…is not only conversion, it is the highest state of the human soul" (*2 Corinthians*, p. 67). For a Christian there's no experience more thrilling than knowing Jesus. There's no friend greater than the Friend of sinners, no relationship deeper than one with the Church's self-sacrificing Husband, no job more fulfilling than being a slave of the Master, no food or drink sweeter than the Bread and Water of Life, no vacation more refreshing than the Rest for our souls, no possession on earth more valuable than the Pearl of Great Price, and no pleasure of sin that's better than the reward of gazing on the face of God's Son. True Christians love Jesus. If you don't love Him, you're not a Christian.

True Christians will continue to love Jesus because of His grace. Thirty years after Paul wrote his letter to the church at Ephesus, Jesus commanded John to write a message to the same church. Sadly, over those thirty years this bride had "abandoned the love [she] had at first" (Revelation 2:4). Yet, Jesus, the church's patient Husband, fanned her love into flame by reminding her of His constant presence and compassionate attention (2:1), by praising her strong perseverance (2:2-3, 6), by directly confronting her problems (2:4-5), and by deepening her anticipation of eternity with Him (2:7). I've found that Jesus uses these same methods with me, especially loving confrontation. Almost nothing increases my love for Christ more than times of repentance when I get a fresh view of His cross and my desperate need of it.

True Christians will never stop loving Jesus. Love that doesn't last isn't genuine. As John says, professing Christians who don't continue in faith were never genuine to begin with (1 John 2:19). However, the fact that you have an *undying* love for Jesus doesn't mean your love is *unwavering*. Your river of love for Christ will never dry up completely, but it may endure periods of drought. Many Christians can tell of long periods of backsliding when they lived in conscious disobedience, often resenting God for the trials He allowed them to endure. If that's part of your testimony, I know that you've found sin to leave scars, and you'd never recommend that anyone follow your example. Yet, you've found God to be immensely gracious and faithful. You've found that He patiently walks with you, and He uses His rod and staff to bring you back onto the path of righteousness for His name's sake. In his classic allegory *The Pilgrim's Progress*, John Bunyan describes Jesus' constant work to keep our love for Himself aflame:

> The Interpreter took Christian by the hand and led him into a place where a fire was burning against a wall, and one standing by it, always casting much water upon it, to quench it; yet the fire only continued to burn higher and hotter. Then Christian said, 'What does this mean?' The Interpreter answered, 'This fire is the work of grace that is wrought in the heart: he that casts water upon it to extinguish and put it out is the devil; but let me show you why the fire, nevertheless, continues to burn higher and hotter.' So then the Interpreter took Christian to the other side of the wall, where he saw a man with a vessel of oil in his hand, which he was continually, but secretly, pouring into the fire. Christian said, 'What does this mean?' The Interpreter answered, 'This is Christ, who continually, with the oil of His grace, maintains the work already begun in the heart. By doing this, even though the devil tries to quench the fire, He ensures that the souls of His people remain in grace.'

Christian, Revelation 2:1-7 shows you why Ephesians 6:24 is true. Your love for Jesus will never die because Jesus Himself will never stop pouring the oil of His grace on your heart.

Let the gospel enflame your love for Jesus even when Satan tries to use trials to douse it.—Joe

"The sufferings of this present time are not worth comparing with the glory that is to be revealed to us." — ROMANS 8:18

There should be a "friendship *faux pas*" list that people have to memorize in order to be admitted into adulthood. Near the top would be *unhelpful* things to say to someone who is hurting:

> *"Well, it could be worse. Count your blessings."*
> *"What happened to you is nothing. One time I…"*
> *"Things are bound to get better."*

Actually, things are not bound to get better. According to 2 Timothy 3:13, there's a very good possibility that they'll get worse. What a happy thought! No wonder Paul described our dim prospects on earth this way: "If in Christ we have hope in this life only, we are of all people most to be pitied" (1 Corinthians 15:19). Thankfully, our hope isn't just for now (though Christ does make life on earth bearable). Our great hope is for the life to come. Contrary to the pithy proverb, time doesn't heal all wounds. Ah, but eternity will! Suffering is our lot on earth—but glory follows! Consider the beautiful promises that plant our hope in heaven:

> So we do not lose heart. Though our outer self is wasting away, our inner self is being renewed day by day. For this light momentary affliction is preparing for us an eternal weight of glory beyond all comparison, as we look not to the things that are seen but to the things that are unseen. For the things that are seen are transient, but the things that are unseen are eternal (2 Corinthians 4:16-18).

> Beloved, do not be surprised at the fiery trial when it comes upon you to test you, as though something strange were happening to you. But rejoice insofar as you share Christ's sufferings, that you may also rejoice and be glad when his glory is revealed (1 Peter 4:12-13; see Romans 8:18).

Keep the end in mind. The burdens we bear now might feel like a crushing weight, but they are light compared to the weight of the glory that is to come. Sorrow endures for the night of our earthly existence, but joy comes with the dawning of eternity (Psalm 30:5). Take courage.

I don't know that I've ever known someone who was as confident of her future hope as Denise, a dear lady at Tri-County Bible Church (Madison, Ohio) whom I was privileged to pastor through her battle with cancer in 2002. Her life was filled with trials even when she was healthy, but cancer made it seemingly insufferable. In an email to me on October 15, 2002, in the midst of chemotherapy (which brought its typical, excruciating side effects), Denise wrote the following:

> The light from my Lord that is within is so strong that all the darkness around me does not matter. This is only for a moment of time. My hope is in the Lord. I will be in a perfect glorified body that will not be limited to any moments of time. Oh, what a glorious day that will be; I shall be in the presence of my Lord, in body and soul and not just spirit.

Those are remarkable words—and true! Denise had less than four decades on earth, and her time was filled with "fiery trials." But right now, at this moment, she is with her Lord. She enjoyed worshiping Jesus from afar; how much more must she enjoy worshiping Him face to face. Her cancer is dead, but Denise lives. Her "light momentary affliction" has been cast off, and the glory that she awaited has arrived. Christian, fix your hopes on the immeasurable joys that are yet to come. I love the way C. S. Lewis captures the wonder of heaven in the conclusion of *The Chronicles of Narnia* series:

> All their life in this world and all their adventures in Narnia had only been the cover and the title page: now at last they were beginning Chapter One of the Great Story which no one on earth has read: which goes on forever: in which every chapter is better than the one before (*The Last Battle*).

Let the gospel make you anticipate future glory as you endure present pain.—Chris

"My brothers are treacherous as a torrent-bed, as torrential streams that pass away." — JOB 6:15

Job's friends let him down when he needed them most. Just like thirsty desert travelers leave the highway hoping to get a drink from the nearby stream only to be disappointed when they find it dried up (6:18-20), so Job was thirsty for his friends' comfort only to find that they added to his pain with their cruel words (6:15-17). How can Christians be like refreshing streams for our brothers and sisters who are traveling through the desert of suffering? Here are three bits of counsel rooted in the book of Job.

Be present. At first Job's friends offered an excellent example of comfort: they were responsive, sympathetic, and "there" (Job 2:11-13). Christian, don't be like many believers who avoid sufferers because it would be awkward or because they wouldn't know what to say. John MacArthur counsels, "Perhaps the greatest injustice we can do a grieving parent [who's lost a child] is to remain silent about the loss that has been experienced.…Even if you only say, 'I'm sorry and I love you'—you will have said a great deal" (*Safe in the Arms of God*, pp. 155, 169).

Admit your limitations. Job's friends had a fundamental problem: they assumed that they could help Job. They thought that they could understand his problem and help him out of it. We often think the same way. Such arrogance makes us either avoid sufferers because we think we need "the answers," or it makes us hurt sufferers when we try to give them "the answers." If you're going to help those who are hurting, you must *admit that your friend needs more than you can give.* Don't have a Messiah complex. Your hurting friends don't need you; they need the Lord. The only voice that really satisfied Job was the voice of God (Job 42:1-6). You must also *admit that you don't fully understand what your friend is going through.* Truly, many trials are common to humanity (1 Corinthians 10:13), and it's helpful to be able to comfort those who are suffering in ways that we have suffered (2 Corinthians 1:3-7). But we must be careful not to assume an arrogant posture of "been there, done that." Even if you've been through something very similar, don't pretend that you fully understand. *Admit that you don't know God's reasons.* We might understand the Bible's teaching on God's purposes in suffering, but we must be careful not to think we know how to apply that to the specific situations of others. We don't know why God does what He does! And even if we have an inkling, God is doing a thousand times more than we could ever imagine. *Admit that you can't predict the future.* Job's friends thought they could predict when God would stop making life hard for Job and when God would begin to bless him again. They were wrong! They didn't have a clue. You don't either.

Ask questions, listen, and learn. When you interact with suffering Christians, approach them as a learner, not as an instructor. Let their example and words (if they're able to talk) teach you. *Ask what's difficult for them.* As you learn about the multiple facets of their trial—physical, spiritual, emotional, relational—you'll discover that you had no clue what they're really enduring. *Ask what God is teaching them.* Job's friends had so much to learn from their godly friend. They should have asked him, "How did you praise God after He took everything? How did you respond without one ounce of bitterness? How have you persevered?" We have much to learn from our suffering friends. If it's true that God does some of His best work "in the dark," then we should assume that our suffering friends have much to teach us. *Ask how they'd like to be helped.* When offering help, it's best not to say, "Call me if you need anything." Instead, ask, "How could I support you right now?" The most meaningful help to those in need costs the comforter a great deal! Jerry Sittser wisely teaches, "Comforters must be prepared to let the pain of another become their own and so let it transform them. They will never be the same after that decision. Their own world will be permanently altered by the presence of one who suffers. It will bring an end to detachment, control, and convenience" (*A Grace Disguised*, pp. 176-77).

These bits of advice strike at our disengaged lives, arrogant attitudes, and clumsy words. If you're a rather pathetic comforter (like me), run to Jesus for forgiveness. If you've offended someone by your words, ask their forgiveness, too (Job 42:7-9). Then, spend much time studying Jesus' glory: He's the Comforter who never breaks a bruised reed (Isaiah 42:3; read Richard Sibbes' classic *The Bruised Reed*). Gazing on Jesus' glory has transforming power.

Let the gospel cleanse you from past unkindness and equip you for meaningful comfort.—Joe

"So to keep me from becoming conceited...a thorn was given me in the flesh."
— 2 CORINTHIANS 12:7

We live in a world of thorns and thistles, part of the fallout of the Fall. Christians don't escape being pierced by thorns. In fact, to read the "trauma log" that is 2 Corinthians 11:23-28 is to understand that the gospel often attracts affliction rather than repelling it. The Christian life is a thorn-filled life.

Of course, Paul goes on in the next chapter to address one especially troubling thorn. 2 Corinthians 12:7-10 doesn't identify the thorn, and it's vain to try to guess what it was. Scripture is ambiguous here for a reason, allowing each of us to apply the text to our own ailments, whether physical, emotional, relational, or spiritual. Whatever is piercing you, take courage from knowing that it's a friend.

Thorns are a means of grace. Twice in verse 7 Paul says that the thorn was intended by God "to keep [him] from becoming conceited." Paul was given awe-inspiring revelations from God. Pride would have been natural. In mercy (that probably seemed like malice for a time), God used the thorn as a "tether" to secure Paul to Himself. God is a master Multi-tasker, but you can be certain of this: He is using your trial to grow you in Christlikeness (Psalm 119:67; Romans 8:28-30; James 1:2-4).

Thorns are a weapon of Satan. Also in verse 7 we learn that Satan intended Paul's ailment to harass him. Satan is sinister. He wants our destruction *now*, even if he's lost us for eternity. Thankfully, what Satan intends for evil is used by God for good. Even as our adversary roars and prowls, he is on God's leash, doing God's bidding. Pray that Satan's schemes will drive you *to* Christ, not *from* Him.

Thorns are a source of strength. Paul was desperate to have his thorn removed. He prayed for deliverance three times—to no avail. God is more interested in *refining* us than *relieving* us. God left the thorn. But with it, He gave *grace* sufficient to endure it. He gave *strength* that would have been unknown without it. He gave *joy* that caused Paul to treasure the thorn as a friend, not an enemy, because it brought him the weakness that unleashed Christ's power.

I close this book with "Friendly Thorns," a poem that grew out of my own trials a few years ago. I trust it will remind you that the burdens you fear will crush you are actually God's gifts to grow you. Grace!

> *For ev'ry branch that's high and green*
> *A root dives downward, dark, unseen.*
> *To stand when furious winds have blown*
> *A tree must cling to soil and stone.*
> *So Christians who would upward grow*
> *Are anchored deep by secret woe.*
>
> *Where tow'ring ships o'er oceans blow*
> *Their heavy ballasts lurk below.*
> *Though lofty masts draw sailors' eyes,*
> *The sunken burdens save their lives.*
> *So we who race through waves and reefs*
> *Are kept upright by hidden griefs.*
>
> *The soul that stretches wide and tall*
> *Must root itself to Christ or fall.*
> *So God of pride and peril warns,*
> *Then tethers saints to Him with thorns.*
> *Thus friendly thorns are gifts of grace,*
> *And uneased pains, His strong embrace.*

Let the gospel give you grace *for* your thorns and *through* your thorns.—Chris